WHAT'S YOUR (ANALYST'S) DIAGNOSIS?
TRUTH (OR FANTASY)?
AN ESSAY ON HUMAN PERCEPTION

WHAT'S YOUR (ANALYST'S) DIAGNOSIS?
TRUTH (OR FANTASY)?
AN ESSAY ON HUMAN PERCEPTION

DR. FRANK E. DAVIS III

ARPress

ARPress
45 Dan Road Suite 36
Canton MA 02021

Hotline: 1(888) 821-0229
Fax: 1(508) 545-7580

Ordering Information:
Quantity Sales. Special discounts are available on quantity purchases by corporations, associations, and others. For details, contact the publisher at the address above.

Printed in the United States of America.

ISBN-13   Paperback   979-8-89389-644-2
               eBook   979-8-89389-645-9

Library of Congress Control Number: 2024921599

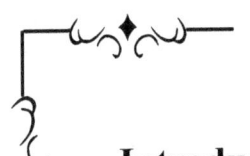

Introduction and Challenge of this Book

This book presents as natural phenomena:

(1) Human perception relates to the truthfulness or fantasy world conceptualization of the primary parent-child relationship. It is possible to "split" human behavior and perception into true or false, using lack of duplicity as to reality and behavior perception, as the measure of true.

(2) The universe, as we know it, can be universally interpreted with the new "Unified Field Theory of Charged Particle Relations and Mass-Energy Transformation". While this is essentially the electromagnetic theory, with a positive direction towards unity of matter ("material") and thought and a negative direction towards randomness or energy, this new name is required to encompass the other theories, atomic and gravitational and to explain inertia as a force.

(3) Perceptual "indeterminacy" results from false superegos and results in feelings for, or "identifications" with, "unknowables", dissociations, or untruths.

(4) Consciousness of truth results from equal focus of consciousness on self and the environment (or object) and results in perception of further truths as to real associations and dissociations. Truth compels perception of the association of true relationships and denies perception of unrelated entities as associative. It specifically denies and identifies untruth. The "academic" reader may find the integration or synthesis of emotion or spirituality in this writing offensive or "metaphysical". Yet, this work illustrates that emotion is always present in perception, especially when that emotional connection is denied. To reveal one's emotional connection should be viewed as more honest or informed than to hide it or appear unaware of it. To express true emotion is to uncover the true spirit. Emotion's expression reveals truth or falsity of the spirit. The soul, always in harmony with nature, is always true.

Challenge: The reader is asked to be the judge as to whether the author has adequately and truthfully presented the case for the above findings of fact. Narcissism (selfishness, sinfulness) is presented as defining the self and objects by fantasy. It is shown to exhibit a "split", not unlike schizophrenia, which inhibits reality perception. Exploration of a perceived "split" in Albert Einstein leads the author to a perceived solution of the "unified field". The solution is, of course, what Professor Einstein anticipated. The reader is asked to examine the author's thoughts and to reach a conclusion as to the truthfulness of the proposed "unified field". Extensive references are given to guide the reader's search for truth. Techniques used to identify truth, by its lack of duplicity, are also presented. This book is an essay on human perception. It is adequately appreciated only when, the real value of true perception, of reality, is recognized.

CONTENTS

Part One

"Normal Science" as Perceptual Reality

CHAPTER I
"Normal Science"

"Normal science" for Thomas Kuhn (1962)[1] "is predicated on the assumption that the scientific community knows what the world is like". It is hoped that the reader does not find this funny! While "knowledge" of "the street" of the "mad scientist" does suggest some scientists are "crazy", any faulty perception scientists have is costly to all of us. The "gravity" of this situation will become very apparent as this book progresses. Kuhn's conceptualization of "normal science" is Einstein's "positivistic philosophical attitude" (Clark, Ronald W. 1971, 1984)[2], and the American Psychiatric Association's "narcissistic personality disorder"[3] with a fantasy world of unlimited brilliance. Clark presents Einstein's "positivistic philosophical attitude" on page ninety as: "The antipathy of these scholars towards atomistic theory can indubitably be traced back to their positive philosophical attitude." "This is an interesting example of the fact that even scholars of audacious spirit and fine instinct can be obstructed in the interpretation of facts by philosophical prejudices. The prejudice – which has by no means died out in the meantime – consists in the faith that facts by themselves can and should yield scientific knowledge without free conceptual construction." On page seventy-seven, Clark presents Einstein as a scientist whose work was "the search for a unity behind disparate phenomena," which had acceptance of a reality "apart from the direct visible truth." This was not denial of truth, but recognition that reality could be different from the perception of truth, or "the direct visible truth". Einstein's use of the word "visible" is not "randomness". It can be related to his proof that light (visible electromagnetic radiation) is attracted to objects, like masses to each other, by "gravity". The line of thought presented here is that recognition of new knowledge can be inhibited by an errant belief that perception is reality. The belief that perception is reality is equivalent to defining reality (world) by perception (self), instead of defining perception (self) by reality (world). Science of discovery, as opposed to "normal science", is a method used to find truths, perceived by some as "unknowable"[4]. So, the "normal science" of Thomas Kuhn is true application of known concepts. While, application of the scientific method is use of truthful observations (that may not be "the direct visible truth") to establish conceptualizations then recognized as science.

This book illustrates how truthful observation is inhibited by the "positivistic philosophical attitude" or the "fantasy of brilliance" of "normal scientists". The intelligent reader should now recognize the real (as opposed to relative) self-defeating nature of narcissism (selfishness). Allowing oneself to achieve a capacity by-fantasy, denies that self capacity-in-reality. A fantasy of "absolute power corrupts absolutely", because it does not require truthfulness of the "power illusion" to reality. This is "original sin". The serpent speaking, "For God doth 'know' that in the day you eat thereof, then your eyes shall be opened, and ye shall be as gods, 'knowing' good and evil".[5] A fantasy of knowing denies one, knowledge, because it does not require what one "knows" to be related to reality. The fantasy worlds are assumption of entitlements not granted by reality. The fantasy of brilliance "splits"[6] perceptions into real and unreal for its own reality preservation. The fantasy of brilliance actually becomes the software of that genetic person's operation and perception of life – a false reality. Frank Elbert Davis, III, M.D., FACS

The following pages illustrate the solution of the structural, developmental, and psychic energy problems of the personality disorders (sinful man-woman syndromes). The reason psychoanalysts have been so unsuccessful in the cure of personality disorders is their own, untruthful, perceptual reality with apparent inability to recognize fantasies or false beliefs in these disorders as superego (parental) in origin. Inability to bring material to consciousness is well recognized by them, for others, as a sign of repression. The material of this book suggests their denial of fantasies and false-beliefs, as superego or parent, is evidence of repression in them.

Making truthful observations, developing true conceptualization, and applying true conceptualization to new experience for its interpretation, are the activity of a true scientist and the personality of a truthful person. This work is not new, novel, or aggressive in nature. Actually, this book could be considered merely an extension of Freud,

Ferenzi, Masson, and others. Freud presented all of this material in his work,[7] but it is divided by Freud's two different states of consciousness. Ferenzi (1932) presented it, as synthesis in his controversial paper. [8]Masson[9] pointed out the duplicity and denial of Freud, yet did not recognize that they were results of Freud's defense of his ego, the state of knowing. Freud made true observations as to traumas, developed true conceptualizations from his observations, and applied these concepts to hysterical patients for cure in at least eighteen of his clinical cases[10]. Yet when he was challenged, his ego as "knowing" could not withstand the observation of other "knowing" people that these hysterics were being "aggressive" towards him. Freud could not explain to his critics that the neutral position was: for him their thought was aggressive, whereas, for the patients their thought resulted from past relationships projected to him from prior objects. Freud's challengers were in denial of the fact that two people with intact capacities of the five senses perceive reality differently because of different prior relationships. Freud's critics were in denial of transference. Freud's challengers forced him to deny his true perception of the psychic reality of hysterics in order for him to preserve his ego state of "knowing", because they could not perceive a superego as separate from the patients or the reality of patients as separate from their own. This is Sheldon Bach's "narcissistic state of consciousness."[11] Freud had to deny his work on hysteria to preserve his self-image of "knowing". Therefore, the loss of his work or its nullification seems to have resulted from psychical reality unrelated to Freud's truthful observations. In fact, Masson's book[12] documents the psychoanalytic community's denial of Freud's clinical data, as well as Freud's denial of Ferenzi in order to defend Freud's ego. Freud's use of the word "dumb" to characterize Ferenzi's paper, when telegramming Eitingon, September 2, 1932[13], actually solidifies the fantasy of Freud as being "brilliant" or "knowing" as opposed to truthful, a self -image he specifically denies for himself in his "Moses and Monotheism" paper[14]. Freud's denial of a truthful real world, in his "Moses and Monotheism" paper, could actually be interpreted as "projective identification[15]" or the belief that the world was, like Freud, untruthful. Freud's projection of "dumb" to Ferenzi is actually a defensive projection of a "devalued" self and is an example of his unconscious.

When it is recognized that this book reports solution of the personality disorders (cause of sin) as delayed due to the "split" of the analytic community's consciousness due to the fantasy of brilliance or "knowing", it then seems reasonable that solutions could be developed to other problems by recognizing similar "splits". Freud originally solved the cause of the personality disorders as due to emotional traumas and later denied that solution to preserve his self-image of "knowing". Einstein believed he had a subconscious perception of a "unified field". There is, at least to this author, a suggestion that the "unified field" problems of Einstein, and others, could be solved by understanding Einstein's self-image as "devalued" and defined by the restriction to his "free conceptual construction" as unable to assume, as a direction, unity. This will be explored, later in this book.

The function of this chapter is to introduce the fantasy world of "knowing" or brilliance as an inhibitor of cognition, or consciousness of real situations, by denial of the true negatives of self. It is not generally recognized that reality states have complements or "mirrors"[16]. For the conscious, it is the subconscious. For the overt it is the covert. For truthful persons, it is the liars. For the subject, it is the object. For the overidealized, it is the devalued. Kuhn's real accomplishment was pointing out that: scientific revolutions result from failure of scientists to recognize what they do not know without crisis. Consciousness of real data, in the physical sciences as well as the social sciences, can be inhibited or blocked to knowledge, because of a fantasy of "knowing" and the ideal self-image as "being in the know", living in the fantasy world of unlimited brilliance. The purpose of this book is to precipitate the crisis (realization that normal science frequently is not in the know) that will lead to knowledge denied by fantasy. This will be a scientific revolution where the fantasy of knowing is replaced by truth of what is known. The illusion of power will become real power.

References to Chapter I:

1 Kuhn, Thomas S. (1962, 1970, 1996). **The Structure of Scientific Revolutions**, Third Edition. P.5. University of Chicago Press, Chicago, Illinois, 60637.

2 Clark, Ronald W. (1971, 1984) **EINSTEIN** – The Life and Times. Avon Books, P. 90. An Imprint of Harper Collins Publishers, 10 East 53rd Street N.Y., N.Y., 10022-5299.

3 American Psychiatric Association (1994). **DSM IV**, Pp. 658-661; Fourth Edition, 1400 K Street NW, Washington, D.C., 2005.

4 Freud, Sigmund. (1938). "An Outline of Psychoanalysis" (P. 196). **Standard Editions** 23: 196.

5 **Genesis** 3: 5.

6 Kernberg, Otto F. (1975, 1985, 1986). **Borderline Conditions and Pathological Narcissism**; Pp. 229, 29-33. Jason-Aronson, Inc. Northvale, New Jersey.

7 Freud, Sigmund. Personality Dissection, Id, Superego, Ego. **Standard Editions**: 19 Pp. 19-39; 22: 57-80; and 23: 195-207.

8 Ferenzi, Sandor (1932). **Confusion of Tongues Between Adults and the Child**. Paper presented at the International Psychoanalytic Congress, September 1932, in Wiesbaden. IJP, 1949. Translation in Masson's THE ASSAULT ON TRUTH below, Pp. 291-302.

9 Masson, Jeffrey M. (1984, 1985). **THE ASSAULT ON TRUTH**– Freud's Suppression of the Seduction Theory (Pp. 107-144). Penguin Books, Viking Penguin, Inc. 40 West 23rd Street N.Y., N.Y.

10 Freud, Sigmund. (April, 21,1896). **The Etiology of Hysteria**. Standard Editions 3: 189-221.

11 Bach, Sheldon. (1977). "On the Narcissistic State of Consciousness". International Journal of Psychoanalysis 58: 209-233.

12 Ibid. 9.

13 Ibid. 9, P. 170.

14 Freud, Sigmund. (1938). **Moses and Monotheism**. Standard Editions 23: 3-137 (129-132).

15 Ibid. 6.

16 Kohut, Heinz (1968). The Psychoanalytic Treatment of the Narcissistic Personality Disorders. Psychoanalytic Study of the Child: V. 23, Pp. 86-113.

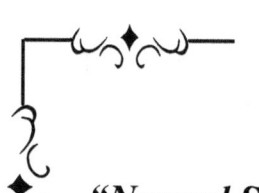

CHAPTER II
"Normal Science," or The Fantasy World of Unlimited Brilliance, as the Psychic Reality of Current Psychoanalysis

The author has previously related the opinion that Kuhn's "normal science", Einstein's "positivistic philosophical attitude", and the fantasy world of unlimited brilliance share the same core identity. This is the identity of self as "knowing". Therefore, when "normal science" fails, it is a result of a "grandiose self image"[1] or a "positivistic philosophical attitude". That fantasy world is now reluctantly projected to analysts who have not reached a generally accepted synthesis as to cause of the personality disorders. In addition to failure to solve this very important problem, the editors of the psychotherapy journals refuse to publish this author's "observed" solution to this problem, despite his submission of eleven "papers" demonstrating its solution! The reason for their failure to publish these "papers" is their lack of emotional perception of their objects. The "transference", "false connection", or "mésalliance", shown in their 'bad self' is their "forbidden wish related to a compulsion to associate which is dominant in their consciousness."[2] This "compulsion to associate" is a "fixation" on a trauma, in this case the self-image of not knowing relative to a dominating parent, that becomes the opposite of the state of consciousness for these personalities or 'character's. This is Breuer's interpretation of "Anna O.' or Bertha Pappenheim.[3] It relates that, this phenomenon, "transference" was first discovered by Dr. Breuer. Now Freud wanted the image or illusion of "knowing". So, he published this finding. Many analysts may believe "transference" is a phenomenon discovered by Freud. Actually, Freud jumped on the "transference" "band wagon" only until it threatened his illusion of "knowing". When he was challenged, he "split his ego in the process of defense"[4], denied the reality of "transference," and projected his hysterical "Three Essays on Sexuality" (1905). This is a digression to explain how the reader can perceive the false "transference" of the editor-analysts to the author of the "papers". The reader should recognize the "real" reason why this author's "papers" are repeatedly rejected is a false "transference". The editor-analysts' responses to the author's "papers" are a projection of their fantasy of unlimited brilliance and the Oedipal complex where they appear to believe the author is trying to destroy them, when his perception is that he is trying to lead them away from duplicity and hysteria.

The author wishes to strongly legitimize the taking of this position so as not to appear to have "feelings of entitlement" that would allow him to assume such a critical point of view. For those students of psychoanalysis, the strongest support for this position would probably be from Freud. Freud clearly believed someone outside the field of psychoanalysis would reach solution to the narcissistic disorders[5]. It may not be obvious that this implies a trait common to psychoanalysts that would block their perception of that solution. Freud also gave strong warning that "egocentrism"[6] and "negative reactions"[7] of the analyst could inhibit reality perception. Einstein and Kuhn have already been mentioned as persons who held the perception that failure to reach synthesis, as to reality, often results from the false belief in "knowing" or having full knowledge. Masson, in his book ASSAULT ON THE TRUTH,[8] documents the psychoanalytic community's denial of clinical data made available to it in clinical sessions as resulting from different perceptual realities for patients and analysts. Masson, pointedly, asks how analysts could possibly know patient's "regressions"[9] to be false. His book and, apparently that of Robert Fliess, are strong supporters of the point of view presented in this book. Why should we, as only peripherally interested parties, assume the reality perception of an analyst's position as to true reality more accurate than that of the person who experienced the situations related in the sessions? This is especially relevant when the father of psychoanalysis has related to us that assuming a truthful relationship with the world is not real or true of the world (See "Moses and Monotheism[10]"). Freud apparently did not realize that Moses, by giving the standard of truth, gave his followers a standard to judge Moses by. Freud did not give his subconscious standard of brilliance for himself. It had to be reached by this author using Freud's technique of analyzing Freud's "free association" in the form of his writings. Aren't the analytic sessions held to explain the patient's reality perception and relate that to real events? Piaget[11] relates the child-like nature of egocentrism and its inhibition of truthful perception. The apparent wisdom of the street is that psychoanalysts are "crazier than their patients". This use of the "common sense" of the street does not give validity to the perception, but that "common sense" perception can be explained by the perceptual reality of this author. The explanation given here is the diagnosis "narcissistic personality disorder with fantasy world of unlimited brilliance associated with a tendency to hysteria" for the psychic analysts. Said differently, their present perceptual reality, as to interpretations, is narcissistic (egocentric or sinful) and untrue. Finally, the author attempts to validate his diagnosis with the demonstration of real behavior of analysts of the three specialties of analysis. The "transference conflict" or "object relation conflict" is that despite repeated and persistent attempts to get the analysts to take a position as to the truth of the identity: Fantasy world = Superego – Ego complex, their response has been "empty", except as to narcissistic defenses and projection of the fantasy of brilliance or "knowing" as true of themselves. This is subtlety associated with an intuitively perceived projection that the author wants something other than the truth from the editor-analysts (they are projecting their hysteria onto him).

Despite these reasons legitimizing his position, the author has been very reluctant to carry this conflict to the larger world. First, this asks a great deal of the world outside the analytic community. The vocabulary and conceptualizations are difficult. There is the possibility that the larger world will take the untruthful, "worldly" view of Freud, a superficial and untruthful view. Yet, the world has a great interest in the usefulness of this true knowledge. The world's response, globally, is unpredictable and is unlikely to be universal. The world has seen similar perception before and reacted with polarity, violence, and murder of some of its proponents. The author speaks of Jesus Christ and some of his followers. The world of reader-patients is an interested party. For, as potential patients, their truthful healing, as opposed to denial of world conditions, is dependent on recognition of reality, not an untrue psychical reality of fantasy. Second, the great respect for and cognizance of the great genetic intellectual abilities of the analysts makes the author aware of his great vulnerability. The ease with which the analysts could simply reproject the author's opinions about them to him should be obvious to all readers. Yet, the whole point of this book is that diagnoses must reflect real events, as opposed to pathological fantasy or perception of analysts. If reprojection occurs, the world should recognize that as "projective identification"[12]. The author is very much aware of the medically and legally granted illusion of power given these persons to declare him "psychotic" or "schizophrenic" regardless of his real state of mind. Because of a marked difference in our apparent perceptual realities, they could attempt to do so. This superficially seems paranoid, until you recognize Freud did this to Ferenzi. Masson gives this full story[13].

The following is the author's presentation of his perceptual reality for the editor-analysts. It is an organized "free association" or "regression" of the author to editor-analyst relationship. This "regression" of the relationship is, for the author, a history of "progression" in his understanding of the Narcissistic Personality Disorder with fantasy of unlimited brilliance and lack of a truthful "superego" (sinful man-woman syndrome of "original sin").

The Diagnostic Criteria: The author will use D.S.M. III and add D.S.M. IV[14].

(1) The grandiose self: The analysts are perceived by the author to have an exaggerated belief in their selves as to the quality of "knowing" or brilliance. The grandiose self they "feel" is at the expense of their patients, generally. But, in the specific transference conflict with this author, their "feeling", as to "knowing", is gained by not recognizing the true value of the knowledge that the fantasy worlds or false beliefs are both ego and superego. Since the therapy of psychoanalysis results from the revelation to patients that the fantasies or false beliefs result from an untrue primary relationship, failure to identify the parent or superego is critical. Denial of this relationship results from the fantasy world of brilliance or "knowing". This denial is evidence of repression of the editor-analysts' primary relationships with aggressor caretakers who perceived self as in the "know" without regard for the real needs of the analysts as children. In the case of the editor-analyst to author

relationship, it is failure to appreciate the "real" author's awareness of something the editor-analysts do notrecognize as the truth, or "know". The "grandiose self" in such personalities is a complement of their perception of truthful personalities as "rigid", because the "grandiose self" results from subconscious invasion of the ego boundary of the "devalued object" and is met with anger, even admitted outrage. This perception of injustice is the stimulus to the statement of victims towards "neutral observers" that, "If you", as a "neutral observer", "are not with me, you are against me", because you do not "stand up" and you allow the "status quo" to continue, as the accepted, unjust and destructive state of affairs that it is.

(2) The fantasy world of unlimited brilliance is the second criterion. The author has just demonstrated revelation of its presence in the "transference conflict". The "needs of the situation" regarding the validity of this demonstration relate to the absolute truth of the relationship of "fantasy world", "world view", ego, and superego as identities. The "needs of the situation", knowing the relationships of the fantasy world or false beliefs to superego, are not met by the analysts' responses and the responses given are provably not true. This documents the fantasy world of brilliance as real and true for the analysts in that it shows it projected as a "defense mechanism".

(3) Exhibitionism is the third criterion. It is broadly defined as the need for near constant attention. Because the author projects the fantasy worlds as superego and ego, it is incumbent that he document that the attention required is focused on the fantasy world of brilliance or "knowing". The author points out that all the time these analysts spend with their patients and in writing papers is attention to, or consciousness of, the fantasy of brilliance or "knowing". This exhibitionism has the function of reaffirming the fantasy world as real. Virtually all the id libidinal energy or energy of the physical person is consumed in the affirmation of the fantasy world. Projection of the fantasy world of brilliance as both superego and ego is required by the theory and truth of "transference" and is notduplicity.

(4) Rage, emptiness, or withdrawal in response to criticism or defeat is the fourth criterion. Readers and, especially patients, should be aware of the apparent "emptiness" of psychoanalysts in "therapy" sessions where they seem to be "withholding" constructive advice and forcing patients

to find the answers themselves. This "emptiness" will be defended as part of the "technique" and it does have some merit. But, their "emptiness" is very similar to their "emptiness" in their responses to my "papers". Read this entire book to see its result. Recognize too, that this "emptiness"could be viewed as a "defense" of the analysts against critism for "not knowing". To project this pattern as part of a fantasy world as ego – superego complex, it is incumbent upon the author to convince the reader that these responses occur, with most intensity, relative to the fantasy of brilliance, or the self-image of the analysts. The "emptiness", "rage", and "withdrawal" exhibited by the psychoanalytic community to Masson's book should be sufficient for any reader. All readers of this book should recognize the "emptiness" of the responses of the editors to this author's "papers". Their responses invariably fail to address the thesis of the author's papers as to truthfulness (showing "emptiness"), "withdraw" from further consideration of the thesis by use of Bion's defense of inhibiting communication[15], and defend the grandiose self as being greatly in demand and needed in more important matters (papers of authors who share the fantasy world of the editor-analysts), exhibiting "haughtiness". The truth is that the personality disorders are among the most costly disorders of our planet, as seen in dollar and human suffering costs, but especially in terms of opportunity costs inestimable because of "unknowing" or "emptiness" as to "knowing". Freud would probably use the word "dumb" here. The author views most people with a fantasy of brilliance as having above average intelligence and expresses reverence for all persons. The author's greatest reverence is for truthful persons. The editor-analyst's "withdrawal" denies them the substance of their fantasy! The editor-analysts will never know the answers to the personality disorders, if they continue to deny that they do not know them, "feel" that they are unimportant or, "are not psychoanalytic"!

(5) Feelings of entitlement are the fifth criterion of D.S.M. III. This is the apparent "feeling" that the analysts have as to "knowing" without apparent complementary requirement that their knowledge be related to real events outside their minds. It appears to the rest of us that these analysts believe they know reality, implicitly. Their fantasy world is that their psychical reality is real, that their perception is flawless. It is a common experience of their patients that these regal feelings of

entitlement have a certain charm. A book could be written about these "feelings" as opposed to reality.

(6) Interpersonal exploitation: In the fantasy world of unlimited brilliance, common exploitation of the object is in the areas of denial and grandiosity. The analysts deny the truthfulness of the author's perception that the fantasy worlds are superego or assume credit for that discovery. Either position is "exploitative", because each is provably untrue as to conscious recognition in the psychoanalytic literature. What would be most classic would be for one of the recipient editors to publish, as his own work, this author's perception of the identity of fantasy world = superego - ego complex. If they deny the identity's truthfulness, they are maintaining that Freud's theory of personality development by superego-ego is invalid, they are denying the "identity" of superego as the "value system" of the person, and they are denying the validity of the theory of transference. If the editor-analysts suggest the identity has already been discovered, they should be required to show, in the published literature, where it says that the fantasy worlds of the narcissistic personality disorders are the superego identifiers for those patients. An example of "interpersonal exploitation" is Anna Freud's assumption of Ferenzi's "identification with the aggressor" "defense mechanism" as her own work.[16] Already pointed out, is Freud's image association with the phenomenon of "transference". Well, which is it "Transference" or "Hysteria"? In Freud's case it is both! Freud "set it up" in the "split of his ego" that he would win either way! To answer Masson's question, Freud had a "split" of his consciousness, due to a need to feel "knowing" and an assumption of "the aggressor" mode as to "knowing". Of course this gave him the "devalued" state of his subconscious of, "Reality will always remain 'unknowable'."[17] It seems to this author, this manuscript has just demonstrated a superego-ego complex of the fantasy of brilliance in successive generations of the Freud family that appears to be genetic, by genes, but is actually "transference of a wish" by verbal conceptualization and "identification with the aggressor"! The author now presents the Freud "Family Value" of "Knowing" by "Interpersonal Exploitation" as a "transference", "false association," or "mésalliance": Freud associated Josef Breuer's perception of the "symptoms of hysteria as determined by certain experiences of the patient's which have operated in a traumatic fashion and which are

being reproduced in his psychical life in the form of mnemic symbols"[18] with his own belief that the traumas were rape. Breuer was reluctant to allow Freud to associate Breuer's name with Freud's "Studies on Hysteria", because Breuer wanted Freud to omit the "sexual factor", because the idea that hysteria was caused by sexual traumas was as repugnant to Breuer as it was to the rest of Freud's colleagues. Freud's use of Breuer's case of "Anna O." led to the dissociation of Freud and Breuer as friends. They never worked together again.[19] It is very important to recognize that the whole truth of this conflict between Freud and Breuer is not known to this author, but does appear to be directly related to the concept that hysteria is caused by sexual traumas of a physical nature. Freud originally held the position that the traumas were physical in nature and, later, that they never occurred. Breuer seems to have held the position that the traumas were emotional (or verbal conceptualizations) and not physical. In that sense, the conflict between Freud and Breuer may be a conflict between Masson and the current author, Davis. That is Freud, initially, and Masson, in his book, appear to have believed that rape or seduction were invariably the cause of hysteria, whereas Davis, and possibly Breuer, recognized the cause of hysteria to be the limitation of conceptualization of a primary "love-hate" relationship by sexual imagery as "love". It is the misalliance of the concept "love" with an unwanted state of sexual submission or victimization that is hysteria in acquisition. The adult's conceptualization of this state of sexuality as love leads the child to "feel" and conceptualize sexuality or sex appeal as love. The parent of same or opposite sex can cause this misalliance, simply by making the untrue, exclusive association of love with sexuality. The "common consciousness" of hysteria is that love is defined by sexuality. Its "common unconsciousness" is that there is no other love. The "common consciousness" of many analysts is the Oedipal complex, a sexually defined relationship. That "common consciousness" defines a "common unconsciousness" of all other types of relationships. It inhibits or obstructs consciousness of the varied asexual natures of love, or the forces towards unity, by a "compulsion to associate" all relationships with the Oedipal complex, a sexually defined relationship. It should be recognized by all reasonable people that a "compulsion to associate" evil or untruth with good or truth is evil, as is, a "compulsion to associate" good or truth with evil.

Misalliance of dissociates is evil! When Freud was attacked and ostracized for his belief in "transference", he then "renunciated the seduction theory"[20] as the cause of hysteria, thereby denying the reality of "transference". He then: (1) projected his "brilliance" as the "Great Man" of psychoanalysis "fusing" himself with the "knowing" people or "those in-the-know" and (2) projected the Oedipal complex for all "unknowing people". This is classic "splitting of the ego in the process of defense"[21] or the "disavowal process"[22]. The reader-patient of this book, surely, should recognize that Freud's "split" and the "split" of the psychoanalytic community determines or "identifies" the egos of each as "belief in their brilliance" or belief in their "state of knowing". Later, Freud developed the practice of psychoanalysis using a "negative" or "mirror image" of "transference", the "Oedipal complex" and "stages of sexual development". The Oedipal complex is a sexualization of all thought processes or hysteria. Meanwhile, Sandor Ferenzi presented his paper "Confusion of Tongues..."[23] which confirmed the true association of "transference" with a reality negative to the feelings of those to whom "aggression" was directed and first presented the "defense mechanism" of "identification with the aggressor". Freud renunciated Ferenzi, calling him "dumb" and "paranoid" with "neurosis"[24]. Ferenzi died a broken man, because of his love of his friend and primal father figure in psychoanalysis, Sigmund Freud. While Freud was quite successful in making himself the primal father figure in psychoanalysis, he was somewhat less successful in his attempt to make himself the "Great Man" of Jewish thought.[25] Anna Freud, Sigmund Freud's daughter, attended the Wiesbaden conference where Ferenzi presented his paper "Confusion of Tongues..." (1932) which gave us the "defense mechanism" of "identification with the aggressor". Anna Freud associated this "defense mechanism" with her name in her book, "The Ego and its Mechanisms of Defense" (1936 and 1966)[26]. She denied Ferenzi credit for the discovery of this "defense mechanism" and continued to deny the reality of "transference", while she exhibited her father's family value of "knowing" or having the illusion of "knowing" at the expense of Sandor Ferenzi. Anna Freud's behavior proves the "transference" of a "fantasy world of brilliance" with "identification with the aggressor" to be real, as if by genes. The real truth is that "transference" is a real transfer of a value system used in the conceptualization of reality whose transfer is accomplished by the spoken word as it relates to specific behaviors such as "interpersonal exploitation". The "Freud Family Value" is the value of their illusion of "knowing" or "original sin". Their behavior in the projection of that illusion is "interpersonal exploitation". That behavior "does violence to the personal integrity of"[27] their victims. The "Family Value" of current psychoanalysis, psychiatry, and psychology is use of the "Oedipal complex" and sexual stages of development to analyze the minds of others. This "generally accepted practice" "does violence to the personal integrity of patients"[28]. This behavior "projects" or "projectively identifies" the hysteria of the editor-analysts to their patients and is a "defective product" in their "generally accepted practice". The editor-analysts' illusion of "knowing" by "interpersonal exploitation" of this author, in their rejection of his "papers", is a rejection or negation of the real author and "does violence to" his personal integrity and to him as a personality. Further, the generally accepted practice of projecting the hysterical "Oedipal complex" to all persons in analysis, and human perception in general, "does violence to the integrity of" our world's true state. The "Oedipal complex" is the "negative" "transference" of hate, lies, murder, and destruction, where sons and daughters envy the power of their parents and seek to take it by murder or fantasy of murder.[29] This is truly one of at least two ways to perceive the universe, but should not be projected to all persons of the universe as to their core behavior. Another behavioral universe is the one of truth, love, life, truthful associations, and construction, as would be truthful conceptual construction or "interpretations" based upon the true facts of given "material". The author of this book expressly forbids the use of this "work product" to sue editor-analysts without his expressed, written, and notarized permission. Any suit brought by editor-analysts relative this "work product" should be interpreted as "interpersonal exploitation" of the author by the editor-analysts with the motive of maintaining their illusion of "knowing" at the expense of the author's projection of true knowledge, or of his "free speech", "free association", and "free conceptual construction". The editor-analysts' use of this "work product" for the purpose of a lawsuit against its author is expressly denied.

(7) Over-idealization alternating with devaluation: The fantasy world of brilliance or "knowing", for the editor-analysts, causes them to perceive objects, patients, and authors as good or "over-idealized" if they affirm the fantasy of "knowing" or brilliance for the editor-analysts or bad or "devalued" if the objects, patients, and authors do not affirm the editor-analysts as brilliant. The fantasy world of brilliance "splits" or "filters"[30] objects, patients, and authors into "brilliant" and "special" or "dumb" and worthless. Note that: the fantasy world can be defended, when the editor-analyst is wrong, by the editor claiming "stupidity"(Bion)[31]. Recognize this as a defense, by fantasy world, of the primary relationship of the editor-analysts or a repression of recall of that primary relationship. Also, see the fantasy world as the identifier of the primary relationship's "interest" or "value system". Recognize the "complementarities" or psychic energy balance of this situation. The "over- idealization" of editor-analyst is "devaluation of author". Any exaggerated "brilliance" for the author would be a "devaluation" of the editor-analysts as "stupid". All we really need is the true facts and the true associations. The author is certainly no more intelligent that the editor-analysts. The author has a different level of consciousness or perception relative to the "identity" of the fantasy world = superego-ego complex. This author's papers have been "devalued" because they do not affirm the fantasy world of the editor-analysts. The problem for the editor-author relationship, as opposed to the editor-analyst relationship, is lack of shared identity with the fantasy world of brilliance or "knowing". The author "feels" he must correlate hisknowing with true observations as opposed to psychical reality or emotional need to be brilliant. Thus, the fantasy world of brilliance is, again, confirmed as the superego-ego complex of the editor-analysts.

(8) Lack of empathy: The author finds the definition of empathy to be "identification of the situation, feelings, and motives of the other person". The history of psychoanalysis, since repudiation of the seduction theory, is "identification" of analysis with the "feeling ofanalysts as knowing" rather than identification of the situation, feelings and motives of patients. In the specific situation where this author presents the identity of: fantasy world = superego-ego complex, there is no identification of the author's papers (personal "situation", "motives") except as to title and their relationship to the editoranalysts'

fantasy worlds of brilliance. The analysts' position relative to depression is often to advise patients to focus their thoughts (consciousness) on parts of their lives not related to their depression. This is a projection of "knowing" without empathy. The needs of the world are certainly larger than the fantasy world of brilliance. The author does not deny the effectiveness of a change in the focus of consciousness as effective treatment of depression. Dr. Burn's book[32] is an excellent book to read when one's reality is unbearable and demonstrates great "techniques" to restore ability to deal with the world. But, the author's broader consciousness is of the true world, as opposed to psychical reality or the fantasy world of the analytic setting. There are real causes of depression for which psychic cures are diversions of fantasy or temporary changes in the state of consciousness. The suggested change in state of consciousness involves denial, a trait of personality disorders. This book makes the point that the fantasy of brilliance or "knowing" is an inadequate response to real problems, showing lack of empathy. Of course the "defense" of their behavior is that, "We are all in the same world". Readers, that is a response that is psychically "untrue" and "inadequate to meet the needs of the situation" and you do "know" it!Readers of this book should recognize that position ("We are all in the same world.") as a "defense mechanism" related to a different psychical reality for the analysts than for the patients. That psychical reality of the analysts is that "knowing" is omnipotence. It is clearly not.

(9) "Believes that he/she is 'special' and unique and can only be understood by, or should associate with, other special or high status people (or institutions)". This criterion is from DSM IV[33]. It implies that there can be a "fusion" between a person and an institution, such as a journal, profession, "divine right", or university. The author believes there is a "fusion" of psychic analysts (to include psychoanalysts, psychologists, and psychiatrists) as to the fantasy world of "knowing" or brilliance. For them, their psychical reality of "knowing" relates to their training and association with others who have some certification of "high status". For this author, their association with others having certification in these fields fuses them in a group with duplicitous perception. In the specific instance of the editor-analyst to author relationship, there has been a recurrent request for the author to obtain the assistance of a psychoanalyst, psychiatrist, or psychotherapeutist

in the submission of the author's papers. The American Journal of Psychiatry requires six psychiatrists to sponsor submission of papers (or they did make that requirement of this author). Such requirements limit or restrict the journals to a reality perception common to persons participating in that specific "normal science". The trait of "inbred" comes to mind. "Inbred" here means a group of people united by a common fantasy related to a common "normal science" involvement. The result: journals that have conceptual fantasies perpetuated as if by genome of the allowed contributors! So that, if all psychiatrists have the fantasy world of brilliance as their ego, from superego conceptualization as by current training in psychiatry, only articles consistent with that fantasy world will be accepted for publication. The "public" then sees the ego trait of all psychiatrists as "knowing" or having the fantasy of unlimited brilliance. The "common sense" view of psychiatrists is that they are "crazier" than their patients. Thus the "special" nature of psychiatrists becomes a shame, rather than an honor. This is an example of the real self-defeating nature of narcissism. They want accolades for their "brilliance", but are viewed as "crazy" because of that very fantasy world of "brilliance". Of course, they are well paid in this "real" world! The joke appears to be on the public.

(10) "Is often envious of others or believes that others are envious of him or her." Again, this is DSM IV. Awareness of truth in a relationship does not associate only one party with having value and is neutral as to envy. The editor-analysts might believe this author is "envious" of their illusion of power as to the truthfulness of his finding that the fantasy worlds define the superego-ego complex. He is not. The editor-analysts' use of the word "disappointed" is a projection to suggest the author's feelings, which might suggest that the editor-analysts believe the author has envy of them. This word "disappointed" is used more than once in their responses, it suggests a frequent feeling of "envy" in them, which they wish to believe the author has, relative to their illusion of power to determine reality. Thus, their belief that others are envious of them results from their illusion that they have the power to define reality, rather than find it like other normal people. The illusionresults from the fantasy of brilliance or fantasy of "knowing." In truthful reality, as opposed to the editor-analysts' psychical reality, the identity of fantasy world as superego-ego complex is true, or not true,

and is unrelated to brilliance, except as to truthfulness of perception. The author now points out that all of the personality disorders share the flaw of disorientation to truth, because "reality" (truth) is defined by persons with personality disorders relative to psychic (selfish) needs rather than truthful situations.

(11) "Shows arrogant, haughty behaviors or attitudes." "Arrogance" and "haughtiness" are shown by the editor-analysts in their assumption of entitlement to "knowing", without consistent support in the literature for the positions they take. In their denials of publication of the identity of: Fantasy world = superego-ego complex, the editor analysts, repeatedly exhibit arrogance and haughtiness. This arrogant, haughty behavior is a direct result of their superego-ego complex as the fantasy world of brilliance or a fantasy world of "knowing", when they do not know. It is their defense of "not knowing". It is assumption of the grandiose self, a controlling and aggressive self that should be "identified with an aggressor," "knowing" parent, the superego-ego complex.

To examine the "defense mechanisms"[34] for this disorder: "splitting" of object (author) occurs due to identification of the author as having the identifier "brilliance" or not. Authors, who project this fantasy effectively, are likely to be published; those who do not exhibit this fantasy, as a trait, will not be published. Identity of the author and fusion of him with his work is preserved by the title of his work with his name. But, there is no apparent effort to justify editor-analyst decisions relative to a reality separate from the psychical reality of the editor-analysts (specifically, the literature relevant to the interest item of the papers). When the author suggests the editor-analysts should use the literature in responding to him or that the editor-analysts should respond to specific questions relative to the origins of the fantasies, the author is ignored. There is an "empty" response. This "empty" response appears to show a "lack of conscience" relative to the literature of psychoanalysis. The superficial and engaging charm of fantasy is "empty" and "boring" compared to the fullness and stimulation of full dimensional unity with the literature and truthful perception. Unity with truth gives Einstein's "magnificent feeling"[35]. All readers should recognize that, lack of knowledge of the psychoanalytic literature is specifically not an identifying trait of psychoanalysts. So this apparent "lack of conscience" actually results from a lack of true identity of the author. It is "obliviousness"[36] to his true feelings, motives, and value system. This "lack of conscience" or "obliviousness" should be recognized by the reader-patients as an inability of the editor-analysts to identify other people with an identity that denies editor-analysts their fantasy world of brilliance or fantasy of themselves as "knowing". To the serious reader-patient, this should reveal the intensity of the editoranalysts' primary relationship relative to the identifier of "knowing". Contrary to the concept that antisocial personalities have no superego, this demonstrates the superego of antisocial personalities to be an intensely held fantasy world that prevents the antisocial personality from perceiving his true object and true self as separate from fantasy. But, the "identification" is also with the trait of subconscious "aggressor". So that, "sucker"1nhas the global trait of non-aggressor, author, patient or innocent reader. Now, digress to the frequent use of the word "sucks" by our U.S. adolescent population. Their use of this word may be "Confusion of Tongues" for our relationships. Possibilities for their meaning are: that they allude to the suckling child who is dependent and needy or weak and devalued by others; or that the object participates in fellatio; or that they view that object as devalued or worthless and use the word "sucks" to defend themselves from perception of hate. If our adolescents use the word "sucks" to defend themselves against the perception of hate, it is certainly not related to a "stage of sexual development," except that, that period in their lives could be when they developed the hate. To return from the digression, in this case the apparent lack of conscience is actually "identification with the primary object as aggressor and with the fantasy world of brilliance". Acquisition of the personality is acquisition of the fantasy world and aggression by the process of "identification". The editor-analysts have "transferred" or made a "false alliance" of the weakness of themselves, as children, to this author!

The author now submits that he has documented by verbal description a truthful diagnosis (for those in the practice of psychoanalysis, psychology, and psychiatry as normal science) of narcissistic personality disorder with fantasy world of brilliance or fantasy world of "knowing". The diagnosis is established by demonstrable objective behavioral criteria separate from the author's subconscious perception.

The behavioral "criteria" are the American Psychiatric Association's "identification" of this disorder. This is not a "definition" or "feeling" of this author, but an image constructed from "real" events that can be demonstrated. It is, therefore, a "real" identity or real "identification". The analytic setting of these professionals is, obviously, a fantasy world model of the universe, rather than a "true" model, because the analysts do not accept their patient's "regressions" as "real". The reader can explore further documentation of this in Masson's book. The future reception of this book will demonstrate that "reasonableness", as to acceptance of this diagnosis, is dependent upon the superego or "core of character" of the individual reader. But, the question of "free will" relates to the question: "Can the individual choose his perceptual reality, or is he/she, forever, assigned it"? This question will be more thoroughly discussed in a later chapter of this book. There is a truthful answer, but those in fantasy worlds do not want to hear it and will "repress" it, if they can!

For those reader-patients interested in a shortcut, commonly used method, to differentiate truth from errant perception, the author now applies Dr. Otto Kernberg's recognition of duality, duplicity, or "surprising contradictions"[37] with regard to perception as the best qualitative route to early diagnosis of this disorder. First is "mutual denial". The analysts are "aware of the fact that their perception" of the personality disorders "are opposite" to the theory of how psychoanalysis works by transference, "but this memory has no emotional relevance, it cannot influence the way they feel now." This is denial of true self and true object. Next is "denial of negation". This is due to repression, according to Dr. Kernberg. In the situation at hand, the editor-analysts repress the association of the fantasies with superego to prevent recall of their own primary relationships. The fantasy world of "knowing" replaces the truth of the primary relationship and the true reality perception of fantasy world as related to superego (parent(s). Finally, "intermediate denial" is "denial of emotions currently felt". This form of denial is seen, in the editor-analyst to author relationship, as haughtiness or arrogance. This is denial of emotions of inferiority, subconsciously felt by the editors, because haughtiness and arrogance are known "defenses" against feelings of inferiority.

23

This chapter has documented, with behavioral criteria, a diagnosis of the editor-analysts that could be confirmed or tested with further observations. It suggests the personality disorder criteria, once met, give information about the primary and future relationships of those persons diagnosed. It emphasizes duality, duplicity, over-idealization of self, and devaluation of others by persons with personality disorders. It may appear to overidealize analytic and therapeutic capacity, while devaluing analysts. Yet the analysts are shown as imperfect, only by their own collective and properly applied discoveries of truth. This chapter is not both an over-idealization of analysts and a devaluation of them. It is a true recognition of their true great collective work and discoveries and their imperfect or false collective behavior. Narcissism is known to be more visible as group or collective behavior than as individual behavior. The group has been analyzed to avoid individual identity and to suggest group behavioral changes. If individuals step forward as leaders, their individual behavior relative to these issues, and particularly their writings, should be closely scrutinized. The problem of this group's behavior has, clearly, been recognized before. It is time for state licensing and certification boards to recognize false transference in these practitioners as malpractice. To protect themselves from charges similar to this, in the future, editor-analysts must develop further techniques to determine truthfulness of patient presentations and assume responsibility for findings of fact used in interpretations. While some practitioners might react to this demand with an "empty" slow down to grasping the facts, this is clearly not going to "meet the needs of the situation". Whatever the response of the medical licensing boards and practitioners, this author should be viewed as unlikely to allow the present condition to continue and unlikely to retreat from its observation. But, there is a real cost to the author, and he believes the world, that he must continue to focus his consciousness on this "negative" problem, when "real" problems of the physical world could be focused upon. The "forbidden fruit" is not actually the apple. It is the belief that one can have within one's mind, independent of God's truth or reality, a knowledge of good and evil, truth or fantasy.

References to Chapter II:

1 Kernberg, Otto F. (1975,1985, 1986), P. 231. ***Borderline Conditions and Pathological Narcissism***. Jason Aronson, Inc. Northvale, New Jersey.

2 Freud, Sigmund (1895). "Psychotherapy of Hysteria". S.E. 2: Pp. 301-305.

3 Freud, Sigmund. (1896). "Anna O." The story of Bertha Pappenheim is actually Breuer's work sent to Freud in a letter and published in Standard Editions II: Pp. 21-47.

4 Freud, Sigmund (1937, 1938). "Splitting of the Ego in the Process of Defense". S.E. 23: Pp. 275-278.

5 Freud, Sigmund (1920). "Beyond the Pleasure Principle". S.E. 18: 44-61 (53).

6 Freud, Sigmund. (1917). "A Difficulty in the Path of Psychoanalysis". Standard Editions 17: 137 –144.

7 Freud, Sigmund. (1938). "Moses and Monotheism". Standard Editions 23: P. 76.

8 Masson, Jeffrey M. (1984, 1985). **THE ASSAULT ON TRUTH–**Freud's Suppression of the Seduction Theory Pp. 107-144. Penguin Books, Viking Penguin, Inc. 40 West 23rdStreet, N.Y., N.Y.

9 Ibid. 8 Pp. 183-185.

10 Freud, Sigmund. (1938). "**Moses and Monotheism**", Standard Editions 23: Pp. 3-137 (129-132).

11 Piaget, Jean (1937). **Principle Factors Determining Intellectual Evolution From Childhood to Adult Life** is from: Rapaport, David (1951,1956, 1959), ORGANIZATION AND PATHOLOGY OF THOUGHT: Selected Sources, Pp. 154-192. Columbia University Press, N.Y. Also from: Factors Determining Human Behavior: Harvard Tercentenary Conference of Arts and Sciences, by Edgar Douglas Adrain, et al., Cambridge Mass.: Harvard University Press, Copyright 1937 by the President and Fellows of Harvard College.

12 Ibid. 1 Pp. 229, 278 (Klein).

13 Ibid 8.

14 American Psychiatric Association's *Diagnostic and Statistical Manual IV, P.661*. Fourth Edition; also **DSM III**, Pp. 315-317. 1400 K Street, N.W., Washington, D.C., 2005.

15 Bion, W. (1967). Second Thoughts: Selected Papers on Psychoanalysis. London: Heinemann, Pp. 86-109.

16 Freud, Anna (1936, 1966). The Ego and the Mechanisms of Defense (Revised Edition), Pp. 109-121, from: **The Writings of Anna Freud Volume II**.International University Press, Madison Connecticut.

17 Freud, Sigmund. (1938). "**An Outline of Psychoanalysis**". Standard Editions 23: Pp. 141-207, (196).

18 Freud, Sigmund (1896). "**The Etiology of Hysteria**". S.E. 3: Pp. 189-221 (192-193).

19 Masson. Ibid 8, Pp. 82-84.

20 Ibid 8, Pp. 107-144.

21 Freud, Sigmund (1937). "Splitting of the Ego in the Process of Defense". S.E. 23: 275-278.

22 Freud, Sigmund (1937). The Psychical Apparatus and the External World." S.E. 23: 195-207 (204).

23 Ferenzi, Sandor (1932). See Masson 8, Pp. 291-303.

24 Ibid 8, P. 170 ("Dumb"), 182-184 ("paranoid"), 182 ("neurosis").

25 Freud, Sigmund. Ibid 10, Pp. 107-132.

26 Freud, Anna. Ibid 16.

27 Ibid 8, P. 133.

28 Ibid 8, P. 133.

29 Ibid 10.

30 Posner, Michael. (2003). An Approach to the Psychobiology of Personality Disorders. Developmental Psychopathology 15 (4): 1093 – 1106.

31 Ibid 15.

32 Burns, David D., M.D. (1980). **FEELING GOOD** – The New Mood Therapy. The New American Library, 1633 Broadway, N.Y., N. Y., 1019.

33 Ibid 14.

34 Ibid 1.

35 Clark, Ronald W. (1971, 1984). **EINSTEIN**– The Life and Times, P. 77. Avon Books, P. 90. An Imprint of Harper Collins Publishers, 10 East 53rd Street N.Y., N.Y., 10022-5299.

36 Gabbard, Glen O. (1989). Two Subtypes of Narcissistic Personality Disorder: Bulletin of Menninger Clinic 53: 527-532.

37 Ibid 1, 31-33 (Denials), 229 (surprising contradictions).

Part Two

Progress in Perception of Reality - Truthful "Identification"

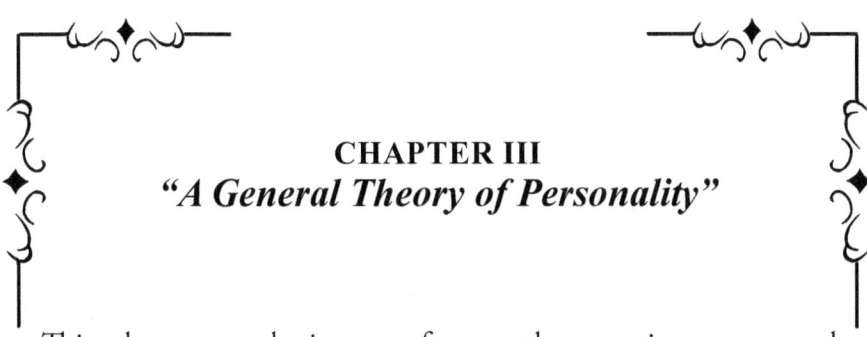

CHAPTER III
"A General Theory of Personality"

This chapter emphasizes, or focuses the consciousness on, the Freudian conceptualization of personality or character development using Freud's inconsistently maintained, but true, findings: (1) This "General Theory of Personality" includes development of normal (true) and abnormal (false) personality and recognizes this developmental process as the Freudian "identification" process[1-6]. (2) If it has not already become so, it should be clear to all readers that the dominant consciousness, or characteristic of personality, is that thought process focused upon in the primary relationship by the "primary caretaker". So that, the "primary caretaker" actually assigns a role or personality (spirit) to the child using verbal and behavioral language to act out and conceptualize their relationship to each other and the world. That each child has his/her own individual genetic (as from genes) characteristics and physical energy force or presence cannot be denied. Also, a given parent may "identify" each child differently with a prior ego "identification". For example, a mother may "identify" her daughter with her deceased mother and "identify" her son with her deceased father. But, the "software" of the use of the child's genetic traits and instincts is "transferred" to the child by the primary caretaker. Freud, in his literature, and the psychoanalytic community, in its behavior, are "ambivalent" on this finding. This "ambivalence" should not be recognized as a character asset. "Ambivalence" is one of the four "A's" of schizophrenia. This author has determined, independently of Freud and the psychoanalytic literature, that "personality", as separate from the genetic person and genetic instincts, relates to "ego instincts" determined in the primary relationship of id ("it" –the genetic entity) to superego (parent and environment). Therefore, a proper "identity" or "identification" of personality and its development is:

World-view (as to behavior and perception) = Superego (parent) to Ego (child) Relationship (as to behavior and conceptualization).

29

This determined "identity" or "identification" as a theoretical "identity" is testable, observable, and verifiable as a true or false theory and is the test of "transference". Many parents wish to deny this "identity" or "identification" process. Clearly, a "negative" identification results from a lack of a proper relationship or absence of parenting. Psychic analysts have "motives" to be "ambivalent" about this "identification process". Yet, it is repeatedly shown to be true and "knowable" with proper search intensity (a requirement of the analysts who may simply be lazy). Step forward, if you wish to disagree. You will be adequately analyzed. Is this "identification" "unknowable" to you? Do you have "ambivalence" as a trait? Do the analysts "identify" with the "ambivalence" Freud exhibited, relative to this process, and acquire his "ambivalence" as "self identification"? Do they have a separate "identity" from Freud. Is this psychoanalytic profession "empty"?

The usefulness of this theory focuses upon truthfulness, reality. To right wrongs or discover untruths, the "compulsion to associate" wrong with right or dissociate truly related phenomena must be eliminated. If wrong is a spirit and right is a soul, "identification" of the right or soul is truth. It is this truthful, loving, and constructive Frank Elbert Davis, III, M.D., FACS process that is the usefulness of this true theory. It focuses consciousness on truthfulness and promotes synthesis of a true self with other truthful associations; its "collective unconsciousness" is lies, fantasy worlds, and dissociative behavior and thought. The focus of such analysis is the finding of all truthful associations, including negative ones that are present, but denied.

"Identification" of the "papers" written in the non-ambivalent development of this book involves a listing of eleven "papers" presented to psychoanalytic, psychological, psychiatric, and natural science journals. While all eleven "papers" were rejected for what are believed to be narcissistic defensive reasons, these "papers" are considered to be very valuable. They are believed to be physical documentation of a scientific revolution in process. Their denial documents the grandiose "knowing" self of the editor-analysts and physical scientists. The "papers" point out the fact that the diagnostic criteria of DSM III and DSM IV project, to readers of them, the object, patient, and "transference" conflicts for each of the ten personality disorders and exhibit the transference conflict as superego. It is only the "narcissistic state of consciousness"

30

which would prevent the analysts from recognizing the object in the criteria as the patient in the original or primary relationship. This results from inability to recognize "transference" due to lack of empathy. The complete "identity" of the editor-analysts is not felt to be required as their "spirit" or superego has been presented. The author surely believes he has presented his superego or spirit. All that remains is listing of the "papers":

To Identify the "Papers":

1. *Theory of Personality Development by Integrational Imprinting*, submitted 2-6-2004.

2. *Narcissistic Personality Disorder – A Lesion of Perception, submitted* 4-8-2004.

3. *Narcissistic Personality Disorder – A Lesion of Perception II*, submitted 4-22-2004. This "paper" associates Koch's Postulates with the fantasy worlds as etiologic agents showing the fantasy worlds to be superego as in the previous chapter's presentation of the editor-analysts. The word "superego" was not yet associated with the function of the fantasy worlds. But, the function of the fantasy worlds was perceived as the etiologic agent or determinant of all criteria, defense mechanisms, and subjective feelings.

4. *Narcissistic Personality Disorder – Fantasy World Structurally located, Superego and the Antisocial Personality*, submitted 4-27-2004. This was actually the author's first written conscious recognition that "the fantasy worlds were the superego". While, papers one and two should have led any reasonable, intelligent, and psychologically trained person to do so, the author did not have the word "identities" of psychology to make the word association of "superego" with the perceived function of the fantasy worlds in the character of persons or "personality".

5. *Narcissistic Personality Disorder – A Synthesis View*, submitted 5-13-04.

6. "*General Theory of Personality Disorders or Theory of Relativity of Truth to Love*, submitted 5-18-04. This paper relates that truth in the conceptualization of a relationship is nearly as important as the love (behavior) of the relationship and may actually be more so for relationship conceptualization.

7. *Personality Development By Object Relations*, submitted 6-1-04.

8. *Psychoanalysis: Seeing Through the "Reality Principle" to Find Psychical Reality for the Narcissistic (Personality) Disorders*, submitted 10-7-04. This paper exposes the analysts as egocentric and relates perception to neuroanatomy and neurophysiology.

9. *Freud and Einstein – 1905-2005: States of Consciousness for Solutions of the Narcissistic Personality Disorders and the "Unified Field Theory"*, submitted to **Nature**, 3-1-05. The reason for rejection of this paper could well be a "Confusion of Tongues…" resulting from use of the term "photon". It could also be narcissism with egocentrism due to a fantasy of brilliance.

10. *Freudian Model– Description of the Narcissistic Personality Disorders– With Clear Structural Identities*, submitted 2-15-05. This paper presents inhibition of consciousness and Freudian structural correlation of fantasy world with superego to ego, relating inhibition of consciousness to the reality that both superego and ego cannot be simultaneously dominant. So that, in the fantasy worlds, consciousness of both cannot be maintained at the same time. This is, of course, the reason for the "narcissistic state of consciousness" or the "false transference" where dissociated phenomena are associated by the "compulsion to associate". This misalliance results from the "defense mechanism" of the primary relationship.

11. *"Identification" – A Positive Perception of the "Negative", "Mirror"-Image "Transference"*, submitted 6-21-05. This paper presents the "negative" "transference" as a photographic negative of the primary relationship due to "identification with the aggressor", similar to Dr. Ferenzi's paper "Confusion of Tongues.." Using concepts like "the logic of relations"[7] and "identities"(as in mathematical and social "equalities") truthfully develops the thought processes. A mathematical equality defines a physical identity or social identity as "relative" to others by the "identity" factor of "transformation" or "transmutation". The mathematical equality is no truer than the "identification" of the real physical or material relationship and its "identifying" factors. The fantasy worlds of the personality disorders falsely enable persons with those disorders to flip their "identity" with that of their objects, as if by a magic wand, due to "identification" with the fantasy world. This is found to be

similar to the use of "transformation equations" in mathematics. The nature of the usefulness of true psychoanalysis should become apparent to the reader in Chapter IV, as Albert Einstein is analyzed using the "technique" exhibited in Chapter II to define the analysts. An "identity" can have positive or negative sign as to truth. Reality determines truth. Truth is not definable. It must be discovered. The "logic of relations" requires all equalities to have similar sign. So, identities of opposite sign do not allow relatedness, while identities of similar sign do. This is true for all defined times and universes as "positions", distances from one another, or physical "identities". "Two wrongs do not make a right."[8] Bad decisions are not excuse for more bad decisions. This leads into Chapter IV. Chapter IV is a presentation of Professor Albert Einstein's "unified field theory". He is credited with its definition, but not its proof. He, as well as any man, recognized a mathematical proof with truthful equivalence of "identities" as indisputable proof of an "identity". Unfortunately, he did not completely present us with that identity. Can we now find the true Professor Albert Einstein and his lost unified field theory? That will require us to solve a problem of the physical sciences with a social science "technique". It requires us to synthesize the true Albert Einstein from his two "split" parts. If we can do that, the accomplishment will be a "Paradise Regained"[9].

References to Chapter III:

1 Freud, Sigmund (1915), "Fixation to Traumas – The Unconscious", S.E. 16: 273-285.

2 Freud, Sigmund (1923), "The Ego and the Id", S.E. 19: 19-27.

3 (1923), "The Ego and the Superego", S.E. 19: 28-39.

4 (1926), "Inhibitions to Consciousness", S.E. 20: 97-100.

5 (1923), "Dissection of the Psychical Personality", S.E. 22 57-80.

6 (1917), "Mourning and Melancholia", S.E. 14: 239-258 (242).

7 Piaget, Jean (1937), "Principle Factors Determining Intellectual Evolution From Childhood to Adult Life", from Rapaport, David (1951, 1956, 1959), ORGANIZATION AND PATHOLOGY OF THOUGHT: Selected Sources, Pp. 154-192. Columbia University

Press, N.Y. Also from: Factors Determining Human Behavior: Harvard Tercentenary Conference of Arts and Sciences, by Edgar Douglas Adrain, et al., Cambridge Mass.: Harvard University Press, Copyright 1937 by the President and Fellows of Harvard College.

8 Bohn, H. G. (1728) Proverbs, P.548.

9 Bohn, H. G. (1728) Proverbs, P.548. 544. The Ronald Press Co. N.Y.

CHAPTER IV
Finding the "Lost" "Unified Field" and the True Albert Einstein

Albert Einstein was adored by the world. He had that certain charm of, "Je ne sais quoi" (Translated: "I do not know what"). But, according to Clark, world fame came to Albert Einstein in 1919 when Sir Arthur Eddington confirmed a prediction Albert Einstein had made about the solar eclipse of September 27, 1919[1]. According to Sir Isaac Newton, to make Einstein's prediction required the "sensorium of God"[2]. Because, when Newton had been asked if gravity was instantaneous, or conveyed at a finite speed, he had responded, "knowing that would require the sensorium of God". Sir Arthur Eddington and others proved the light from foreign stars to bend as it passed our sun during an eclipse. Einstein made this prediction in advance. This successful prediction suggested to "knowing people" that Einstein had the "sensorium of God". To this author, he is loved, but has an inversion in his perception of his negative critics, of his atomic theory proof, when he refers to their attitude as "positive" or the "positive philosophic attitude". Albert Einstein exhibited a clear "devalued" selfimage relative to others and to his favorite intellectual subject, light. This analysis results from reading Ronald Clark's book.[3] Professor Albert Einstein's superego-ego, relative to his work on solving the "unified field", was, "You must not assume unity as both an origin and a direction, you must prove it". His general attitude, when asked if we would ever probe "The Secret" was, "We shall know a little more than we know now, but the real nature of things, that we shall never know, never"[4]. His motive was, "I want to know **His** thoughts. The rest are details"[5]. Now, Albert Einstein seems to have failed to complete his equation because of a few simple errors, because he subconsciously did not want to do it, or because of the "special nature of Albert's circumstances"[6]. This actually seems paranoid, but is it possible he had "The Secret" and did not want to give it to us? Well, it would be better to identify him as schizophrenic than to say he withheld "The Secret" from us. Globally, his ego of not assuming unity as a direction or origin was his core character error. Focally, his error was over-idealization of his object, light. He clearly knew, by the mathematical "proofs" or mathematical "identities" that you have to have a starting point and that determines direction, if you have a goal. He clearly knew about "free association", because his "free conceptual construction" is an "identity of thought" with "free association". But, he did exhibit the error of thought, discussed in Part I for other personalities, that "scientific truth must be conceived as a truth that is independent of reality,"[7].... There is a very subtle difference between this and perception of "a reality that is apart from the direct visible truth"[8]. The difference is the relationship of reality to truth, or not. Truth can be directly visible or not, but it must be real. Perception can be real to a person or true of a person and not represent true reality. Clark relates that Einstein said, "When I relate my methods of thought I come to the conclusion that the gift of fantasy has meant more to me than my talent for absorbing positive knowledge."[9] The reader may now have "flashbacks" to Chapter II. Is this as painful to the reader as it is to this author? This perception of a reality of the mind instead of a reality of the universe is different from his prior words and relates to his self-image or "identity" by definition, rather than "identification" by reality. This is duplicity of his consciousness! Thus, he has a "split" self where he cannot assume something he believes in (and has proven), but he can believe in any thing he "feels right" about. This relates to the terrible stress of his marital relationship and his second son's schizophrenia. The author suggests schizophrenia is a disjuncture of thought or disorientation relating to a lack of relativity of sound conceptualization, or verbal description, to visual phenomena, so that verbal-thought-concepts are not true of reality or visual concepts, but relate to emotional feelings of another person (superego, parents). The disorientation is perceived to be caused by an outside voice, because of that other person's inversion of position and verbal description of reality. To repeat, the foreign voice is an untrue superego due to inversion of position or perception. Since schizophrenia has times of sanity, the proximal cause of the disjuncture is negative environmental stimuli or stress. Schizophrenia is a loss of reality perception by perceptual inversion related to past untrue audible or verbal-thought interpretations (conceptualization of reality) and current, unbearable stress. Similar thought errors are known to be present in the "ambulatory psychoses" or personality disorders. For personality dysfunction, that voice can be the voice of self in the case of a primitive superego and results from a devalued self, not schizophrenia. The reader-patient might think this author is suggesting Albert Einstein had schizophrenia. He is not! He does recognize personality dysfunction. This author recognizes a close relative, common to both the professor and his son, whose study would be very interesting and does not imply genomic etiologies! A definitive discussion of the "sacred feminine" is beyond the scope of this book. The author has not examined Professor Einstein's son's particular circumstances with any depth. Chronic personality dysfunction is personality disorder. The author makes no real diagnosis for Albert Einstein. But, the reader, author, and all other persons, to have a clear perceptual reality of this universe, must look closely at the thoughts of Albert Einstein and make determinations as to truth. We all have free speech, free will, free association, and free conceptual construction.

The author has made a very global diagnosis of psychoanalysts. That group's perception of the author is very unlikely to be positive, because his assessment of them in their area of ego interest is negative. The author exposes them as negative in their belief that the ego has as its conceptual origin, the id. The id is merely the energy source that is directed by the superego value system. Their opinion of the author is, therefore, likely to be negative. Now, since the author believes, strongly, there is a "unified field", he must show similar negativity in the physics community to prove the existence of the "unified field". It would be especially useful to him in his vindication relative to the psychoanalysts if his psychoanalytic impressions would lead him to the "unified field", because this would show an effective consistency or synthesis of truthfulness in his thought process. Of course that consistency would be his ego in operation. So, the author puts himself at risk or makes himself vulnerable when he exposes his thought process in this manner. Later in this chapter, the author will give the reader the ego and alt ego of Albert Einstein, as presented by Clark. At this time, the author wants to relate two relationships of Wolfgang Pauli to show the author's belief that at least one of the physicists share the same narcissistic fantasy world as the psychoanalysts. Now, if the author can show that some physicists have the same lack of consistency or lack of synthesis in their assessment mechanism or process for people as the psychoanalysts, the support for the author's credibility in the psychoanalytic assessment is a support of his credibility in his belief in the "unified field", because the psychoanalytic theory is that the same character or superego value system (mind character) is used in approaching science as is used in approaching people. The core "identifier" is duplicity or "over-idealization" alternating with "devaluation", as in "over-idealization" of self and "devaluation" of object. It is interesting that in psychoanalysis the subject of study is called the object and the self of the analyst is called the subject. Does that tell anyone that they may have things backwards? It is actually the "mirror" image of the thought process. To return to Wolfgang Pauli, Victor Weisskopf, noted U.S. physicist for developing the "Weisskopf formula" for the "single proton theoretical rate"[10], said this about Wolfgang Pauli, "It was absolutely marvelous working for Wolfgang Pauli. You could ask him anything. There was no worry that he"(Wolfgang Pauli) "would think a particular question was stupid, since he thought all questions were stupid." (Physics, Zitzewitz, P. 577)[11]. To analyze this, the author suggests that this impression of Pauli "identifies" Pauli's ego, from Weisskopf's perspective, as "devaluation" of Weisskopf's brilliance, "over-idealization" of Pauli's brilliance, and from this author's perspective, defensive of the fact that Weisskopf might ask Pauli a question that Pauli might not know. If this is the "character" of Wolfgang Pauli, we should be able to see it consistently. Clark presents Pauli in answer to the question of whether a "unified field" would be synthesized as to perception, said unequivocally, "No. What God hath put asunder no man shall ever join."[12] This author analyzes that statement of Pauli and gives the reader this opinion: "This is negativity. This is 'over-idealization' of Einstein in a mocking, hostile, envious, manner. It is a lie on its face with the assumption of either God or Einstein. It puts Pauli's opinion above both God and Einstein's existence. It is a double negative in attempt to assert a positive, that Pauli is brilliant." The author hasn't let Weisskopf off yet. But, maybe, the reader would rather analyze Weisskopf. (Hint: look for over-idealization and devaluation together. Find the conflict and the way the ego deals with it and you find the ego. Is the statement truthful in a spiritual as opposed to superficial way? Is Weisskopf giving us the true Pauli in a loving way?Loving of whom or what?).

Let's look more closely at Albert Einstein's thoughts, as related to us by Clark. He said, "The purpose of my work is to further this simplification, and particularly to reduce to one formula the explanation of the field of gravity and the field of electromagnetism".[13] This statement implies one equation to explain mass-energy transformations and exhibit awareness of both gravitational and electromagnetic theories. The more modern "unified field" concept suggests the need to unify all three theories: gravitational, electromagnetic, and atomic. Albert Einstein conceptualized a theory and developed half of its "identity" as an equation. Along the way, he obtained the Nobel Prize. Professor Robert A. Millikan received a Nobel Prize for confirming some of Einstein's work. But, can we use Albert Einstein's "split" to reach the "unified field"? That is, by studying Albert Einstein's thought process, can we extend the libidinal power of his life? Can the reader see that process as an appreciation of his soul and spirit? It is important to the author that the reader-patient see this process as an act of love, not hate.

Albert Einstein's inability to recognize that he had solved the "unified field" resulted from his "split" of self by two mutually excluding superegos. Said differently, the real Albert Einstein could not function well with two "selves" that were mutually exclusive. Albert Einstein's two superegos were:

(1)   "God is real".

(2)   "You cannot assume unity as both origin and direction."[14]

These superegos were obtained from his words, as related by Clark. They suggest the pre-psychotic state of the "borderline personality disorder" (a diagnostic conceptualization using DSM IV criteria as abbreviated to superego–ego and transference conflict as a complex, not strict criteria) or the narcissistic personality disorder with a fantasy world as superego. The reader will note that "borderline personality disorder" is not a diagnosis given by this author. The severe rage seen in the "borderline personality disorder" is not ever presented by Clark, as an observed trait of Albert Einstein. But the two mutually exclusive superegos of Albert Einstein, given above, are very similar to:

(1)   "Love is real."

(2)   "You are evil" or, "You do not exist". Quickly I say, "This is impossible! We know Albert and we love him!"

The very phrasing of Albert Einstein's second superego is a denial of his real accomplishments. It is a lie on its face. It is a denial of his "unity" of "self". It is a denial of his fantastic work in the field of physics. It is a denial of his pleasant and loving nature. It is a denial of the loveable, adorable, funny, charming, rumpled, selfeffacing real ALBERT EINSTEIN!

Clark presents Newton[15] in his "Optiks": "Are not gross Bodies and Light convertible into one another, and may not Bodies receive much of their Activity from the Particles of Light which enter their composition?"… "the changing of Bodies into Light, and Light into Bodies, is very conformable to the Course of Nature, which seems delighted with Transmutations." Kohut used this term "Transmutations"[16] in his description of the nature of narcissism. A "transmutation" or "transformation" can occur in nature or in the mind and can be effected by a mathematical operation.

Einstein, similarly from Clark[17], "suggested all mass was merely congealed energy; all energy merely liberated matter." Einstein had proven that light energy is affected by gravity. His second superego denied the reality of himself. Since light is affected by gravity, its energy has an equivalent "mass". The critical problem was his "self-devaluation" complemented by the "over-idealization" of the "photon". A "photon", as Einstein quantified it, is not a "particle" as he named it, but is a one second "wave" of electromagnetic "particles". What we have here is "Confusion of Tongues.."[18] This is an inversion of perceptual reality of the "particle" and "wave" by definition as to quantity of energy per "particle". It was a "transmutation"[19] of perception that required "transformation equations". 1-30-06: While it was not apparent to the author at the time of first writing this paragraph, Albert Einstein's choice of the size of the photon, rather than finding it, leads to misperception of "particle" and "wave" from this point on! Likewise, his lack of perception of the "equivalent charge" of "neutral masses" makes it impossible for him to explain gravity in terms other than, "deformation of space". The questions should be raised, "Deformation of space by what? How? Is that a force? Does not physics require **real** physical explanations of **causes** of deformations?" His split of self is the cause of his inability to write:

The Equation of the Unified Field Theory

(For the atom(s)): $\Delta^{Mc2} = \Delta E = EADn \times -EADe = EADn \times EADm \times c^2$ = EADn $x^{+/-}$EADc at velocity c (with sign dependent upon direction + towards a mass or position in question)= [For Gravity]: $^{1/2}$(G((M1M2/ d1²) + (M1$\triangle$M2$\triangle$/d2²))) ^{x} Δ^d = (For Electromagnetism): 1/2(K((q1q2/ d1²) + (q1$\triangle$q2$\triangle$/d2²))) x Δd [For Gravity and Electromagnetism] Δd is positive when decreasing. Perception of the EAD1 as a "particle" is intuitively apparent when thought of as "mass" or "charge". But when the EAD1 is thought of as energy, it is intuitively perceived as a "wave", even though it is only one "particle".

This equation or identity is to be read: "A change in mass times the velocity of light squared equals an opposite change in energy, equals a change in units of energy transformed times the energy of each unit, equals a change in units of mass times the mass quantity of each times the velocity of light squared, equals the energy of the number of unit charges at velocity c, equals average gravitational force times the change in separating distance, equals average electromagnetic force times the change in separating distance." The times and positions of the study, or focus of consciousness, must be determined by the objectives of the study or focus of interest. But the basic tenet is that there is conservation of the matter-energy total, unless matter or energy comes from an outside source not appreciated in the original universe as defined by the "needs of the situation" (study), or the pertinent, relevant, and necessary facts (material). For all mass, charge, or energy in motion, quantitative "equivalence" can be calculated and, for a given determined universe, summated to a constant, dependent on the universe properties as to states and quantities. Said determined universe can change over time by influence(s) from outside the previously determined universe which come into its boundaries. But, all mass, energy, and charge of an adequately defined universe can be known or is "knowable" to an absolute quality and quantity of the EAD unit. The universe, as we know it, operates according to the electromagnetic theory with equivalence of charge in motion, mass in motion, or energy in motion relative to other charge, mass, or energy respectively and there are equivalent transformation factors for the transformation of each to the other, which have been observed in nature. There is an equilibrium of mass and energy that relates, directly or inversely, to time, temperature, and position as related to other "mass", directly or inversely.

"Unified Field Theory of 'Charged Particle' Relations With Mass-Energy Transformation"

Mass, Charge in motion at c, the speed of light, and Energy are related directly or inversely by the equation identity above, and show the properties of global units or "waves" and single units or "particles". 1. A "transformation" is a real change of state of matter-energy, particle or wave and should not result from a mathematical operation, because that would be inversion as to "particle"-"wave" state or properties by thought instead of by nature. Charge in motion at the speed of light is equivalent to mass and/or energy, and is, as an EAD, the exchange value unit-quantity of both. Matter is not energy. Energy is not matter. But, after transformation, one becomes the other. They can be considered quantitative "equivalents" and behave as if they are "identities" in true associations with those respective "identities". Loss of motion of a portion of an electromagnetic wave's particles results in creation of "mass". Mass forced into motion creates energy. Energy is "anti-matter", because $T.E. = K.E. + P.E.$ (Mass) and $E = - (Mc^2)$. The author is unaware of where it might be written in the science or mathematical literature that use of "transformation equations" in the interpretation of data is misleading. But, he wishes to suggest use of "transformation equations" is "observational inversion" or "mathematical inversion to unreal (fantasy)". Whereas, use of unity "identities" can be useful in computation of equivalent values of different qualities when equivalence to a third unity value such as a dollar amount or force amount can be found, as is true for the forces of gravity and a Coulomb's force related to Mutual Atomic-Molecular Polarity (MAMP) or charge equivalence of "mass".

2. The smallest unit of energy is the EAD. The EAD has "equivalent mass, charge, and energy". $EADm = {}^{7.372419 \times 10^{-51}}$ kilograms (Previously copyrighted as "the K" now noted as Kd), $EADc = +1.602 \times 10^{-19}$ Coulombs, $EADe = 6.626 \times 10^{-34}$ Joules or Planck's constant for one EAD, a single "particle" of electro-magnetic energy. The velocity of all of these "particles", when part of an electro-magnetic wave, is the speed of "light" or the velocity of all electromagnetic waves in space

and when not, results in mass from energy. An EAD has only two directions (velocities) relative to or unrelated to any defined mass: (+) Positive, towards the mass and (-) Negative, away from the mass. Since an EAD is received by matter as a charged "particle", and in motion, it has only two axes of "vibration", unlike a "wave" (of particles, photon of one second of particles) that has three dimensions in space. Where the photon wave is approximately 10^{15} particles or 1,000,000,000,000,000 particles (one quadrillion particles) per second, the EAD particle is one particle in approximately $1/10^{15}$ seconds. The photon is a line of EADs or particles one second long, like a column of one quadrillion soldiers. The "wave" nature of the EAD is due to perception of its multiple properties as electric and magnetic radiations ("strings") perpendicular to each other, with the magnetic wave effected as gravity and the electric wave parallel to the propagation by geodesic curvature and effected as electromotive force, inertia. The author has recognized that the EAD has the same charge properties as the "positron" or anti-electron. The anti-electron or positron has much greater mass or energy than the EAD. But, the EAD can displace an electron from its' energy level by entering the complementary "valence band"[20]of an atom or molecule.

Diversionary Discussion

The reader may be stunned at the enormousness of "The Equation's" implications, and for that reason, distrustful or very cautious in the acceptance of the EAD unit. In a book on perception, as well as physics, it is important to present the perceptual process. "The Equation" and the EAD are "identifications". The reader's acceptance of the book as truth should be dependent on this author's ability to convincingly communicate the "identities" involved, so that the reader will have no doubt that the "identifications" given are true ones. The author has reason to believe, from more than one source, that finding the "unified field" is promoted as the main goal of physics today. This concept of the "unified field" is a real concept, consciously recognized but not proven by Einstein, and at least subconsciously recognized by others. Thirty-nine years of Einstein's life were spent in the determined attempt to develop "**The Equation**". His concept of the "unified field" is somewhat more restrictive than the generally accepted concept now, which is to unify gravitational, electromagnetic, and atomic theories. Clearly, to this author, the "photon's" perception as a "particle", rather than as a "wave", was the proximal cause of Einstein's problem. Also, Einstein did not recognize the positive charges of light and positive charges of "neutral mass". This apparently results from ambivalent acceptance of Maxwell's work on wave properties and how they result. To examine Clark's biography, is to find dual perceptions as to whether Einstein used Maxwell's work. This conundrum is what one would expect when Einstein's thought is closely scrutinized. But, let's now focus consciousness on (or give hypercathexis to) the EAD. This is "identification" in process. As of 10:32 A.M. 1-19-06, it is not a complete "identification". But for a reader with a strong ego for truthfulness, the following process should give sufficient reason for agreement with the author that the EAD is a real "particle" despite its existence "apart from a direct visible truth". First, recognition of the EAD as a unit or "particle, where the "photon" is a quantum, bundle of energy, or "wave", comes from the reality and conceptualization of "frequency". Frequency (f) is the number of occurrences over time and is given as number per second. So, the energy of an EAD is h or Planck's constant, as to energy, because Planck found the maximum energy of photoelectrons versus frequency of light to be a constant. With the EAD and photon, we are talking about light, not electrons. So the energy of a single EAD or "particle" of light is h, or actually the energy of h, since h is given as energy per event or per "particle". This fact of the difference between the EAD and Planck's constant proves Einstein's longvoiced and well-publicized opinion that it is an exaggerated or "positivistic philosophical attitude" of the self that suggests that if all facts are presented they will be interpreted to give all true information. It is the author's belief that the question as to whether Planck or Einstein discovered the light "particle" has come up before. Factual interpretation is just as important as the facts. Thinking time or hypercathexis is essential. "Thought experiments" are equally important to knowledge as they lead to conceptualization or synthesis of the factual information. The energy of Planck's constant is given per hertz or number of times per second. (The author notes here that neither Planck nor Einstein associated positive charge(s) to photons or light "particles", even though it is well established that the negative zinc plate, to which the photons go, is neutralized by ultra-violet light (EMRs). Quantitatively, the relative change in charge, from negative to neutral, is related to EAD number, as well as lack of electron potential (negativity) at the zinc plate. This is the "mirror" perception of current flow or wave flow of energy, as opposed to electron flow, a phenomenon not believed to occur at c, the speed of light. The theory of particle electrodynamics (PED) views the "photoelectric effect" as transfer of energy from positive (+) to negative (-), not transfer of mass (electrons) from negative (-) to positive.) So, Einstein's "photon" is a "wave" of events one second long. The EAD has energy equal to the energy part of Planck's constant. This has been the thought process of discovery of the EAD. To put it in the form of an "identity equation": EAD "particle" = Energy of h (Planck's constant or 6.626 X 10-34 Joules)21

A.   To Calculate "Mass" or "Equivalent Mass": (1) $E = Mc^2$. (2) $E/c^2 = M$. (3) M = 6.626 X 10^{-34} Joules/

(2.99792458 X 10^8 meters per second)^2. This gives 7.372419 X 10-51 kilograms.

B.   To Calculate "Charge": (1) One EAD moves one electron through 6.626 X 10^{-34} Joules. (2) Volts = Joules/Coulombs. (3) Coulombs = Amperes/second = 6.242 X 10^{18} electrons. (4) 1 EAD = 6.626 X 10^{-34} / (1/ 6.242 X 10^{18} Coulombs) = 4.1361 X 10^{-15} electron volts. (5) 1 EAD = 6.626 X 10^{-34} Joules/ (1.606 X 10- [19] electron volts/ Joule) = 4.1361 X 10^{-15} electron volts. One Joule is one coulomb pushed over one volt: Joules = Volts X Coulombs. (6) 6.626 X 10^{-34} Joules = 4.1361 X 10-[15 -15] 19 Coulombs. Thus, charge was "identified" to be the same as for a "Positron"! The identity of charge to that of a positron was recognized as the author was working on several objectives at about the same time. Such an electromagnetic energy wave that would appear to be a positive charge would result from perpendicular motion to said electromagnetic wave by an electron at the source of the electromagnetic wave's generation. Charge complementary wave to particle (EAD as electromagnetic wave to electron's particle motion) is recognized as a real physical phenomenon by Maxwell (1873)[22]. Planck's finding that the maximum energy of a "photoelectron" is a multiple of a constant and the frequency of a light wave determined the energy of a single electromagnetic particle. The number of particles equaled the frequency. So, Planck's constant is merely confirmation of the Law of Conservation of Energy. The determinant of Planck's constant is the limit of the speed of light, an upper limit determined by Einstein. To express Planck's finding in the form of an equation:

4.136 X 10^{-15} eV/Hz (h) X Frequency of Light (f) $\geq$4.136 X 10^{-15} eV/Hz (h) X frequency of electrons or $hf_{light} \geq hf_{electrons}$ (Where the electrons are photoelectrons or energy particles)

This equation, above, and the equation, below, illustrate Einstein's transformation of the energy of an electron's charge in-motion to that of a mass in his "Electrodynamics of Moving Bodies" and his loss of mass-energy orientation, as well as wave-particle orientation by the mathematical transform: $Mc^2(1/(\sqrt{(1-B^2)} -1) = hf-w1^{-footnote}$

The energy that Planck's work is referring to is the energy of a "photoelectron". The difference between a photoelectron and an electron is that the energy of a photoelectron should be properly associated with the wave form image or mirage of an electron's acceleration, not the physical "mass" of the electron! This is similar to the difference between electrons flowing in the radio antenna and the electromagnetic wave they generate and should be recognized as two different manifestations of the electron.

The EAD is a positively charged electromagnetic particle with wave properties of electromagnetic radiations that puts "holes" in the atom as an "insulator" and adds energy to the electron wave form equal to its' mass-energy. It is able to enter the "valence band" only if it has a certain minimum frequency that gives it shorter wavelength. When the "photon" makes a "hole" in the atom as an "insulator" for one second or the EAD makes a "hole" in the atom for one second/frequency, if the electron escapes the recipient atom receiving the photon's excess energy, that electron's energy (by Planck) equals the difference of the photon's energy for one second (or the EAD's energy for one second/frequency) and the energy required to "liberate" or "free" the electron and: By Arthur Compton's Effect[23](1922): 1st photon's energy = e shell energy change + 2nd photon's energy (if the electron does not escape).

There is charge and energy conservation with this explanation. This author predicts it will satisfy "energy balance" with fusion also. Further, the suggestion of the atom acting as an "intrinsic semiconductor" is further development of the "atomic theory" and further "proof" of the positive charge of the EAD "particle" or (+) charges of the photon wave equal to f, positive charges equal to frequency number. It is the recognition of the EAD, as being a positively charged particle with an associated wave of energy which displaces the electron to higher energy levels by filling a "hole" in the lower energy level and exchanging energy with it, that proves the EADs properties as real. The light particle does have "wave" properties with a "wave" of energy and a charge of "particle". **Finally**, the author has made an association of "energy with wave of the particle" and "charge with ^{Ellis, C. D. (1944). Encyclopaedia} ^{Britannica, V. 17, P. 788.} energy of the particle". Energy, charge, particle, and wave (mass-energy) are united. The increased mass of the atom with an EAD positive charge and energy gives the total changed mass of the EADed atom to a quantitatively determined mass, energy, wavelength, and charge determination.

It should be clear that increase in mass, that occurs in light absorption, is due to gain of a positive charge equivalent in the "hole" of the valence electron shell and its associated energy is coupled to electron acceleration. Actually the EAD and electron trade energies in an elastic collision where the electron goes out further from the nucleus and the EAD, with its "parity" to the other charged particles of the valence shell, fills the "hole".

To establish the EAD's relationship to matter is to recognize that all matter has a positive charge related directly to its mass. To recognize that an EAD, positive by charge (negative by energy), can occupy a "hole" in the "valence band" of an atom or molecule and displace an electron, suggests "parity" of EADs and electrons, as does the fact that EADs and electrons have a "mirror" property of charge and a perpendicular property of energy direction at the propagation and absorption sites (sites of fusion and energy absorption). To focus on the charge of "neutral mass" as positive and the charge of an EAD as positive, is to recognize that matter has energy as a part of itself and positivity as part of itself. Unity of the positivity of charge and the negativity of energy is the EAD. Thus an EAD is different from an electron in mass, but has an energy "parity" relationship of complementarity in atomic function by charge. That is, the direction of propagation and direction of vibration of an EAD is paired and complementary to that of a conjugal complementary electron. Thus, an EAD enters an atom or molecule perpendicular to the direction an electron leaves it, transferring the EAD energy to it by "mirrored" or complementary frequency. Since frequency is an oscillation of energy (electromagnetic), energy can be exchanged at its aphelions, without loss, to a "paired" charged particle (electron). Since frequency is perpendicular to the line of propagation, the exchange of energy is the exchange of the magnetic energy and the path of exit of the electron or the path of its acceleration is perpendicular to the path of the EAD. The direction of exit of the electron is determined by the EAD's axis of vibration-frequency and then-current vibration direction. To correlate, quantitatively, the positive (+) charge of neutral masses and the EAD: "Neutral mass" has a positive charge of 8.61646×10^{-11} Coul./kg. The EAD is positively charged and is 1.6022×10^{-19} Coul/EAD. So, "neutral mass" has 5.3779×10^8 EADs/kg. The nature of gravity is the magnetic forces due to paired responses of mass related charges. The nature of inertia is the resistance of charge to motion, because of charge relationships to other charged masses or masses of charged 'particles". Inertia is an electromotive force. The positive charge of "neutral matter" is but one face of the two-faced nature of matter. The negative charge of matter is the electron or energy face. These faces are not in opposition when properly synthesized, but lead to the unifying force of gravity, the unity of matter, and this material thought. Gravity is the result of the magnetic force of two masses "linked" together by the complementary positions of their electrons "relative" to their own protons, but also, all the other electrons and protons of the universe and the integration of the charge-force relationship, especially as related to motion and centripetal acceleration. The EAD is related to charge, position, and "mutual atomic-molecular polarity" ("MAMP"). The atoms, molecules, masses, and energy are all mutually polarized, just, as we know their charges are "related" or dissociative, attractive or repulsive. Matter, in equilibrium, is in complementary vibratory equilibrium with energy and the direction of energy is positive (+) towards mass and negative (-) away from it. Mass losses of EADs are energy gains of EADS. The EAD is the unity factor of mass and energy. Energy becomes mass by transfer of EADs from the energy state to the mass state and is synchronous with loss of EAD velocity from c (the speed of light) to that of the mass. Mass becomes energy by transfer of EADs from the mass state to the energy state by acceleration of the EAD to c. Field strength is relative energy of motion of the two masses divided by separating distance squared and is not a constant. The unifying constant of the "Unified Field Theory of 'Charged Particle' Relations and Mass-Energy Transformation" is the energy associated with Planck's constant and the equivalent charge of a positron, the "EAD". It is the unity element of gravity, electromagnetism, and the atom(s).

To make an analogy of the EAD transfers is to view an EAD like the superego. They are present but must be perceived "apart from a direct visible truth". They can be objectively perceived and have been, subconsciously. Large dense masses, like houses and dense stars, have less electromagnetic radiation (EADs) from them because it takes more energy to escape their unity of mass (by Newton) or charge (by Coulomb). Spectroscopy is the objective way to perceive radiated electromagnetic waves.

The EAD does not have the mass of an electron, only its mirror of charge quality (+) and equal charge quantity (1.6022×10^{-19} Coulombs). At this point the author would like to request introjection of a perception that is not completely developed and may be untrue: "It appears that the 'neutrino' is an energy 'wave' and not a 'particle' and is related to the energy of EADs and the photon."

3. Neutral molecules have an "effective or equivalent charge" related to their mass and an "equivalent energy" at rest or in uniform motion. The "equivalent charge" is the universal charge to neutral mass constant, $Dc(8.61646 \times 10^{-11}$ coulombs /kilogram). The " equivalent energy" is the "equivalent energy" in one kilogram of mass ($8.98755178737 \times 10^{16}$ Joules). The mass to charge ratio is the inverse of the charge to mass ratio. Mass to charge and charge to mass ratios are not equal for all "particles", because some "particles" have charge at rest. Since "neutral mass" has "effective charge" dependent on mass, mass in motion is charge in motion and has a magnetic field perpendicular to its motion and an electric field in the direction of its motion. This electric field relates to inertia and the magnetic field relates to gravity.

Calculation of the Charge **Constant Dc**: Charge of a "Neutral Mass" GK = $6.673 \times 10^{-11} Nm^2/kg.^2$ = F =$8.988 \times 10^9 \ Nm^2/Coul.^2$= CK Coulombs^2= $8.988 \times 10^9/6.673 \times 10^{-11} \ kg^2$ = $1.34692 \times 10^{20} \ kg.^2$ Coulombs = $\sqrt{1.3469204256 \times 10^{10}}$ kg. Coul. = 1.16057×10^{10} kg. Of "neutral mass" = + **8.61646×10^{-11} Coulombs/kg. "neutral mass"**

4.   "Particles" and other entities can have different mass/charge and charge/mass ratios except as "identified" "equivalents".

5.   Waves have different frequencies of energy units. Electromagnetic waves have EAD density or intensity at a specific location that equals f, frequency. EAD(s) have a point of origin and move in straight lines, unless affected by gravity, and maintain their frequency, determined by source. Whereas, waves of EADS "particles" have a mass-energy equivalent of origin and disperse as a wave h f t (Planck's constant x frequency x time). The frequency of a point of reception equals the frequency of a point of transmission, but the wavelength is c (velocity of "light") dependent in space and dependent on current medium when not in space. Frequency, or "particle" quantity over time (actually wave) is constant as to energy source. Electromagnetic wave "particles" (EADs) are subunits of the one second "particle" of Einstein (actually a wave, photon).

6.   For any real universe, entities, time, and positions can be determined with true "state" "identities" as to "wave" or "particle", mass or energy, time and position.

7.   According to the, now named, "Einstein Certainty Principle", a change in position or state requires a change in time. This is required by the limit of v to c, a finding of Einstein.

8.   "Mutual atomic-molecular polarity" of "neutral masses", moving associatively or dissociatively, generates the force known as gravity and the second force known as inertia. This can also be called "MAMP", because it is this charged "particle" relationship of "mass" that results in the electromagnetic wave or field of gravity and force of inertia. The electric and magnetic fields are the result of electron position "parity" resulting from electrons associated with masses with a complementary conjugal charge average position relating to the sizes of the masses and inversely relating to the separating distance squared. "MAMP" is the polarity of two masses' relationship by charge due to electron shifting. The charge positions complement each other by "parity", like two electrons in one shell. This is an extension of, or further interpretation of, Maxwell's wave mechanics equations and field theory[24] and an application of the Coulomb force[25] equation: $F = Kq1q2/d^2$, where $K = 8.988 \times 10^9 \ Nm^2/C^2$

9. Gravity can be thought of as "equivalent" to mass-to-mass (wave) attraction or charge-to-charge (field) attraction by "transformation" of real equivalent identities because charge and mass are "identified" as dual identities of matter or mass. "State" (as to wave or particle) must be consistently maintained for the equal force determination. The "mass" of objects as exhibited in "gravity" is the wave generated by "Mutual atomic-molecular polarity" (MAMP) or the equivalent charge, Dc X M. Einstein saw gravity as a "field characteristic of matter"[26]. This "field characteristic" is the wave nature of "equivalently charged" "neutral masses" and their relationships as discussed by Maxwell[27] and Coulombs Law of charged particles. "Identification" by charge or "charge equivalent" of mass is dependent on particle nature relative to other "identified" particles, but is a real "identified" charge in the motion state or codetermined "identity", a conjugal complementarity of mass. To say that "mass" does not have an identifiable associated charge or **charge "capacity"** is to be in denial of the known force of gravity and the known force of attraction of "neutral mass" for all charged particles. It is to leave the explanation of the phenomenon of gravity to an association with a "deformation of space by mass", when most physicists recognize "mass, is not a force" but, is force divided by acceleration. The association of gravity with mass, instead of force, and the dissociation of inertia or inertial state from mass is to have a mental transformation of true physical realities.

10. "State" as to place and time must be defined for the universe in study. Using the same equation, with deltas before each equality, recognizes perception of events from outside the "defined universe". Negative, as well as positive, changes of total mass, energy, or charge at c, to a given universe must be recognized as real.

11. There is a "mirror"[28] of positive and negative universals where positive is "real" and constructive of matter and negative is destructive of matter or real material thought relative to any truthful value system. This is not a defined quality, because "truth" is observable as motion towards unity for mass (material) and negative as motion away from unity. Failure to recognize unity as the positive direction of construction of matter appears to result from the "collective consciousness" and focus of consciousness on the positive proton nuclei of "particle" atoms, rather than the global wave character of atom-molecules,

which appears to be the "common unconsciousness". Truth in the construction and interpretation of this material reflects recognition that each statement has real truth on its own, or not, and therefore positive or negative value. The equation: $E = Mc^2$ is often "interpreted" to mean that mass and energy are equivalent when actually these entities give equivalent quantities for transformations which occur in nature. When recognized as an equivalence of transformation, mass and energy are dissociative, rather than related directly, and it is through this dissociation that transformations occur. It is the egocentric state of consciousness (duplicity) that fails to see that, if mass and energy are related by the equation $E = Mc^2$ and no mass or energy is added to this defined universe, mass and energy are opposites as to direction and inversely related by c^2. Mass and energy, while different, go through transformation by a matter-energy unit of charge at c, the speed of light. The smallest matter-energy unit (EAD) is true of both matter and energy, but incompletely defines either, except as to quantitative equivalence. It relates to matter (mass) in positive direction as if mass, to charge as if charge, and is energy as charge in motion with direction. Failure to recognize "transformation" of energy to mass (matter) in the absorption of light by an atom causing electron centrifugal acceleration and increased atomic polarity is a denial or unconscious state of perception for: (1) effective mass resulting from atomic polarity and (2) the effective positive charge of light. A given universe (or subject of study) can lose mass-energy (or material) from its boundaries by negativity.

12. "Truthful" can be a single motion of nature or a single decision determining direction by the observer. "Truthful" is found, not defined. Truthful positivity is towards unity of thought and unity of matter and unity of both with perceptual reality.

13. The "real" unity of the truthfully-observed universe is so uniform in function as to suggest its form, state, properties, processes, and their relationships, are not random but universally or generally determined as if by some "compass" or directing agency with power and organization. The term "God" has been applied to such direction, power, and organization. This unity is now recognized to follow the electromagnetic theory and the electromagnetic theory now unifies itself, the gravitational, and the atomic theories to form a **"Unified**

Field Theory of 'Charged Particle' Relations and MassEnergy Transformation(s)".

14. A loss of motion or capture of electromagnetic energy "creates" mass by transformation with the EAD as its unit quantity. A gain of motion to electron waves by acceleration of them from (light) electromagnetic energy "creates" mass. "Creation of mass" by electromagnetic energy is "effective Mass" and is the increased atomic-molecular polarity resulting from the addition of the energy with its attendant increased electron-proton distance and EAD positive mass. The direction of "creation" of mass and energy are inversions or conjugal complements. Thus energy is "anti-matter". Electromagnetic energy is generated by: (a) motion of "neutral masses" (actually "paired" neutral masses resulting in relative charge due to "parity");(b) outside physical force or; (c) deceleration of electrons. All three of the above physical phenomena produce EADs or electromagnetic radiation. Planck's findings[29] on "black body radiation" are explained by: The deceleration of electrons with the production of electromagnetic energy results in energy production by a change in the size (mass) of the atom in quantum amounts due to size of "energy levels". The electrons of a "black body" (incandescent light wire) fall from a higher energy level by the release of EADs particles (or photon waves) of light. When it is recognized that the gain of electromagnetic energy is the exact loss of electron energy, it is perceived that what Planck's finding of maximum energy for escaping photoelectrons relative to frequency proved is the Law of Conservation of Energy. Arthur Compton[30] stated the complement of this finding when he pointed out that the energy of photons that accelerate electrons but do not eject them, then have energy equal to their previous energy less the energy imparted to the electrons. While Planck did not realize it, his finding that maximum energy of escaping photoelectrons related directly to the frequency of light as a constant, determined that light energy is directly related to its' frequency or light particle number. Planck was apparently thinking of light as a global "mass" of light with a characteristic frequency. He did not perceive the frequency of the wave of light as made up of many frequency "particles". Einstein perceived the "particle" concept as a one second wave of determined frequency and by this conceptualization lost the real "particle", the EAD. The problem here is the same one

we have encountered in psychoanalysis. The data of Planck[31], and the regressions of patients in psychoanalysis[32], are being misinterpreted due to egocentrism and a belief in "knowing"[33]. Planck's data, showing that the energy of a photoelectron is directly proportional to the frequency of light transferring that energy, should reveal to everyone that the mass-energy of a single particle of light or electromagnetic energy is a constant! The constant energy of that "particle" of energy is the energy portion of Planck's constant. So, the energy of an EAD or single particle is the energy of Planck's constant. While, the energy of a one second wave of electromagnetic energy is Einstein's photon. **The EAD is the mathematical "identity" of the determined unit of electromagnetic energy**, not the photon. Roger Bacon (circa 1250) recognized the value of such mathematical determinations, "If in other sciences we should arrive at certainty without doubt and truth without error, it behooves us to place the foundations of knowledge in mathematics." But, the energy maximum Planck found for a photoelectron is caused by the limits of a reality determined by Einstein, that c (velocity of light) is the maximum attainable velocity. Planck discovered the EAD, except for its charge, and did not interpret his data so as to consciously recognize his discovery. Einstein over-idealized the light "particle". Planck apparently thought the molecules of a solid vibrate when heat or energy is added to them. It appears that molecules of a solid expand their electron orbits, or in effect increase their molecular size, as would be expected with **"The Unified Field Theory of Charged Particle Relations and Mass-Energy Transformation(s)"**, by expanding their electron orbits to higher energy levels. This is a transformation of energy from the environment to effective mass by increasing "MAMP", mutual atomic-molecular polarity, and is energy lost from the atom-molecule to the environment when the electrons return to lower energy levels. The entire molecule is not moving; it is the electron-proton distance that changes. This is a real difference of solids from gases and liquids and is a result of "congealment" or crystalline molecular structure. This is similar to mass getting larger with increased energy from "photons" or EADs. Light energy and electric energy of heat in the light bulb similarly affect the electron orbits of the metal (black body). The increase in length of the metal rod with heat is a well-known and frequently measured phenomenon. It is related to increased electron-proton distance. It is the conjugal complement of a decrease in rod size with extreme velocity and, at c, giving loss of all mass to energy. Equilibrium exists when (P.E.) M = E (K.E.) and is determined by c, the speed of light and probably other factors such as temperature and mass density due to other separate masses nearby (giving a pressure-like phenomenon of EADs escaping and an entropy phenomenon of EADs being captured by complementary masses). "Equilibrium" is when net EAD is zero and is graph able as a "real" quantity, for every instant, with a spectrophotometer surveying of the universe studied. At "**equilibrium**", for any mass defined as potential energy and energy defined as kinetic energy, **PE = KE. T.E. = P.E. + K.E.**

15. A large change of mass to energy occurs with "fission" or "fusion" of nuclei of particles and results from reaching "critical mass" of nuclei in fission and critical potential energy (critical mass) in fusion. Recognize here that, this theory of "particle electro-dynamics" or "charged particle relations" views potential energy as mass. So, "critical mass" is the highest possible "potential energy" state in the observed universe. Critical energy is the highest possible kinetic energy state for an observed particle in our universe and relates to particle velocity at c (the velocity of light – a natural limits constant determined by Einstein). "Fission" can be thought of as "fusion" to reach critical mass by addition of neutrons by critical energy. These critical points are "transformation points" at the extreme positive (mass) and negative (energy) sites on the "real" graph of mass-energy states. These points seem to be fixed by c, the speed of light, the total of PE + KE, pressure, temperature and possibly other "details". It is clear to most "observers" that these points are very unstable. Energy intensity, like matter density, has a certain "critical level" beyond which it transforms to its conjugal complement, mass. This is fusion of energy into mass. The fusion process consumes energy to reach critical mass that then releases energy to a more projectile state. Energy intensity is energy frequency at the particulate level or position in consideration and results from frequency of EADs at that point location during the period in consideration. This frequency of energy at given points in the universe considered is not universally consistent, but is an equilibrating factor, like Brownian motion. Local events of association or dissociation of energy or energy

transformations relate directly or indirectly to equilibrium factors of the associated waveforms and/or nuclear integrity.

16. Energy (Kinetic energy) and Mass (P.E.) are negatively related, because they are mirror complements where KE + PE (Mass) = Total Energy. This inverse "relativity" is now (7-03-06) errantly expressed with the equation: $E = Mc^2$. To denote real directions for mass and energy, this author adds a negative sign to his equation, because energy is perceived as "anti-matter" or "anti-mass" in any real or limited universe. A negative relationship is not a non-relationship, because association of negatively related qualities and quantities can be mathematically equated as above. Because of the "balance of nature" or the existence of equilibrium states, negative relationships have positive conjugal complements. This is where opportunities lie! This work requires extreme care to avoid inversion as to thought. No one should feel shame for the occasional inversion of thought, but persistent inversion after adequate presentation of "identifications" is "rigidity".

17. The transformation equation says that matter and charge in motion at c (energy) are "identities" that are interchangeable except for sign. A loss of one is a gain of the other. But, both entities are true to an absolute fixed amount (unity amount) for any fixed time, place, and state. The total matter plus energy (unity amount) is constant for any instant or event defined as to time, place, and state. There is a determinant factor of change, the EAD. The "Heisenberg uncertainty principle" results from the expected "confusion" between wave and particle that is a direct result of defininga wave as a particle rather than determining the true quantitative value of the particle. The photon is a one second wave of EAD particles (approximately 10^{15} particles). The energy of an electron is real only when an electron is a particle and not part of a wave of a distinct mass-particle. That is, it is improper to describe an electron as having variable energy, when it is part of the "mutual atomic-molecular polarity" of an atom or molecule where energy is constant in "conduction bands". For then, the "energy" becomes "mass" or part of that molecule's polarity, that gives it its' dipolar charge or magnetic quality perceived as "mass", by the likes of James Clerk Maxwell. The error here is denial of the "transformation" of "energy" to "mass". The transformed EAD or photon energy is not merely associated with the electron particle, but is associated with the

atomic-molecular complex of "mass". Bohr's description of angular momentum as "quantized" to $Mv = nh/2\pi r$ demonstrates the indirect relationship of momentum to position (r) and the indirect relationship of energy to time with v as d/t. There is no indeterminacy, because any loss of EAD energy to electrons is gain of energy to those electrons or to the "mass" of the atom-molecule complex. The "uncertainty" is simply the question of whether the energy, h (EAD light particle), is "mass", as part of the atom-molecule, or energy as part of the light wave or as a characteristic of a "freed" electron. The whole situation is certain or "determinate" and follows the Law of Conservation of Mass-Energy. The "energy" is electromagnetic or that of the "freed" electron, the "mass" is part of the atomic-molecular polarity. The "mass-energy complex" allocates the given energy from the EADs entering the situation to mass of the atom-molecule, mass of the atom-molecule and energy of the "freed" electron, or mass of the atom-molecule and energy of the escaping EADs or photon. But there is Conservation of Mass-Energy! Further, the "mass-energy complex" allocates energy towards mass production so that the Second Law of Thermodynamics is violated in this "transformation", because the direction of the energy is towards matter production or mass and unity of matter, not randomness or "indeterminacy". Actually, since the Laws of Thermodynamics apply to energy, and there is a change of state to matter, there is not technically a violation of the Second Law of Thermodynamics. The "mass-energy complex" leads to the further "synthesis" or unity of matter and energy, when light of sufficient frequency strikes matter. While "randomness" is lessened by the unity of matter and energy, stability or equilibrium is increased. "Uncertainty" results from duplicity or "confusion", not knowledge. "Uncertainty" is lack of truthful perception of the nature of the situation. It is the perception of the situation as, either "mass", or "energy", "wave" or "particle", without adequate determination as to which quality it is. It results from a denial of "transformation" in nature. There is no "indeterminacy", because any loss of EAD (photon) energy is gain of mass-energy to that mass, to that mass and its' electron, or to that mass (as mass) with different subsequent photon energy. The precise time of exchange can be determined by disappearance or decrease of EAD frequency, perception of mass increase by polarity (magnetism), or measurement of the electron's energy to a "free" mobile state at a determined velocity. Any denial of determinacy is denial of the "Law of Conservation of Mass-Energy" for an adequately determined universe where scientists are oriented to real quantities of "mass", "energy", "forces", "inertia", "acceleration", "deceleration", "charge", and qualities of "particle" or "wave" and direction "relative" to a given "mass" as "positive towards it" and "negative away from it". "Indeterminacy" is not a result of inadequate tools. It is a result of insufficient work on the part of the workmen! Truthful orientation is the criterion for perceptual reality in physics and all mental states and is not a mathematical operation or one that can be concealed by mathematics (A new form of Bion's[34]"defense mechanism").

18. There are different states: matter as atoms, matter as organized material, energy as "particles" (EADs), and energy as a wave (hf). The special "wave" of one second of electromagnetic energy is the "photon" (formerly thought of as a "particle"). Visible proof of the energy of particles, as "identified" by a wave, is measurable with a spectrophotometer, which detects and graphs the wave or frequency relative to time of electromagnetic waves. E = hft. The single "particle" of e-m energy is the EAD. Global energy becomes all of the "EAD"s or (EADn). Total matter plus energy in an adequately determined universe without changes from outside that universe is a constant so that T.E. = K.E. + P.E. (Mass – In Particle Electro-Dynamics P.E. is mass).

19. The true "logic of relations"[35] is an absolute real quality of relatedness or unrelatedness as to space (position), time, and state in nature, when mental perception, as projected, duplicates nature. "State" can be wave or "particle", mass or atom, truth or lie of perception. The "state of matter" can be an illusion of transformation in mathematics, as in a continuous graph without the "steps" of quanta, or with "transformation equations". Thus, if transformation equations are used, the NATURE of the natural situation or natural state can be perceptually changed by a pure math or a pure false alliance "logic of relations" function that reverses or mirrors nature! "Relativity" requires a true "logic of relations". "Relativity" relates inversely as to distance squared, from unity of matter (or material), and, therefore, position, in space and time. Just as Professor Albert Einstein said, the problems of the "unified field" "relate to" space, time, distance. To assume a perceived "neutral position" or lack of "charge" for "neutral masses" made up of

charges and in motion relative to each other is to be unconscious of a true relationship of "charge" to "neutral mass".

There are many things we do not know about the world and even more so about the universe. But, readers, "truth emerges more easily from error than confusion"(Francis Bacon). Can you see that Freud and Einstein have given us Ferenzi's "Confusion of Tongues"? They made errors we need to have in our consciousness! The author is about to do a detailed analysis of the reasons why Professor Albert Einstein did not reach the "unified field" equation. The emotional pain perceived by this author, at this moment, is almost unbearable! This is the pain felt because of the professor's misunderstanding of himself and the universe. It is the pain of a great "Paradise Lost" and is felt for the professor, even in his absence. The fine professor's core values and abiding feeling, that the "unified field" would be found, were true. Yet his self-devaluation was harmful to everyone. To be truthful and to convince everyone of the truth of this book, the author must analyze Albert Einstein's thought and allow us to grow through that "regression". The reader should recognize that this material is being presented similar to Part I of this book, where a "regression" leads to progress in our thought. Instead of the author's "papers", we will be talking about thoughts expressed, as related by Clark, and Einstein in Clark's book and Einstein's "papers". A great deal of credit should be given to Dr. Sandor Ferenzi[36], Piaget[37], and Masson[38]before proceeding. The author has recognized a reason why Einstein was loved, possibly more than he should have been or "over-idealized". Albert Einstein had a subconscious "grandiose self" hidden by his overt "devalued self". This "grandiose self" was not in the consciousness of the Professor and not in this author's consciousness until the author recognized the "devaluation" of James Clerk Maxwell's work. The readers and the author should recognize that grandiosity must always accompany devaluation to maintain psychic energy balance. Einstein's failure to find the "unified field" resulted not only from his definition of the photon as a wave one second long, but also from failure to find "mutual atomic-molecular polarity" or Maxwell's polarity of molecules, giving magnetism (gravity) to neutral molecules. This was a "devaluation" of Maxwell and an "over-idealization" of Einstein's self. (1) The professor's miss-steps relate to "Confusion of Tongues", as related to Dr. Ferenzi's work, and to the naming of the photon and its perceived "identity". It is probably true that someone other than Professor Einstein named the photon. The "photon", as now accepted in the physics literature, is one second of light of a given frequency or its' equivalent electromagnetic energy. This turns out to be many EADS or "particles" of "light". Planck's constant times the frequency of light yields the current "photon". But, Einstein's original conceptualization of the "quantum"[39] of energy was for one "particle" of light. He "over-idealized" the "photon". He also used the term "bundle" of energy to refer to one "particle" of energy. Generally, or globally, this is a "Confusion of the Tongues" with inversion of perceptual reality and true reality.

(2) "Over-idealization" of the photon causes devaluation of the frequency "identity" of the EAD and loss of the wave identity of the "quantum" or photon, so that, the particle and wave nature of light, as well as its charge, are "lost". This conceptualization is both a "devalued self" (Einstein) and "over-idealized child" (photon). But, it could have been recognized as a "devalued" James Clerk Maxwell and probably would have been, except that Maxwell died 11-05-1879. This is noteworthy for two reasons: First, because it has taken so long to recognize this "devaluation"; second, because of the very real phenomenon that, the devalued person is often the only one to realize his devaluation. The weak positive charge of an EAD is shown by proper interpretation of observations. Two realities prove the real presence of a very weak positive charge for an "EAD" (a) "EAD"s pull electrons away from positively charged nuclei or attract electrons. (b) When you observe that an EAD has energy, discovery of an "equivalent" "charge" allows it to be "mass-less" and move at the speed of light. Assignment of an "equivalent mass" or "charge" allows you to explain the gravity phenomena of light in its curves past the sun in eclipse and in its shift towards the red bands when escaping dense stars. This should be recognized as solution of an "identity problem" of physics as to the full identity of a light "particle" with very small mass and charge, large energy, and two planes of vibration, one of which can be perceived parallel to the direction of propagation by geodesic curves and the other perpendicular to propagation by complement or parity. The author agrees with Professor Einstein in suggesting this is perception "apart from a direct visible proof", but it is actually "free conceptual

construction" where all available data as true "identities", are used to solve a puzzle. The act of "free conceptual construction" is almost identical to "regression and synthesis" of psychoanalysis. There is a disassociation of all material as to facts from interpretation or conceptualization due to some "misalliance" or failure of the old conceptualization to explain new findings. Then the material or facts are synthesized to fit the facts and the real current situation in a manner that continues to explain the earlier situation from which the earlier conceptualization was developed. The "EAD" and "MAMP" explanations of light, gravity (with inertia), magnetism, electron positioning, and atomic structure are all improvements over the Einstein conceptualization and marshal the data more truthfully and completely. It should be easy for the reader-patient to see that conceptualization is dependent on the "position" of the observer or "egocentrism". Some times, it is actually helpful not to have too much information. It is hoped that the reader can recognize that the author solved this puzzle by looking for "splits" and a solution that "fit the needs of the situation" with sufficient, necessary, and all readily available data. Of course, an EAD is one light "particle. "EAD" actually stands for "Elizabeth Anne Davis", but it might be convenient to think of it as "extra analytic detail". This use of the EAD initials is certainly by permission. The particle, "EAD" with energy h, times its number gives all electromagnetic energy for a given event in a defined universe and can be used to "perceive equivalent mass". The informed reader will remember use of "transformation equations" in the Special and General Theories of Relativity. This is another "split". Einstein alternately denied that Maxwell's work influenced his "relativity" and at other times suggested Maxwell's work was one of the three or four most influencing factors in the development of "relativity". This duplicity in Einstein's thinking shows in his conceptualization of relativity and its lack of synthesis for both gravity and inertia. While Einstein did "compulsively associate" or "relate" (as in "relativity") his perception to reality with "transformation equations", he did not see the real relationship of "charged particles" with "neutral masses" as explained with this work using Maxwell[40,41] (1873) and Coulomb's Law[42] (1785). The concepts of "valence bands" and "conduction bands" actually explain the attraction of "neutral mass" for charged particles of either charge quality. In fact this work suggests charge quality (+ or -), for a given mass, is determined by direction of charge motion as relative to or dissociating from that particular mass. Einstein, in his "grandiose self" mode, had "free conceptual construction" that allowed him to propose "relativity" not in agreement with real physical explanations except with similar "flexible" thought processes. This author names the complement of this "split", "mutual atomic-molecular polarity". The term, "mutual atomic-molecular polarity" (MAMP), refers to the phenomenon that all electrons and protons are charged and relate to each other with attraction, or inter-dependently, regardless of distance. This is the physical cause of "gravity". This is also the physical cause of "inertia". To explain, to accelerate a mass or particle that is made up of charges is to cause electro-magnetic force waves to be created (electromotive and magnetic). This is "transformation" of physical force to electro-magnetic force. It is because mass related charge number causes both gravity (magnetic) and inertia (electromotive) that the "coincidence" of their equality occurs. These forces are shown to be caused by charge relationships and to be part of the balance or duality of nature. It is helpful to view this as a change from the physical to the spiritual! It is a transformation that is "apart from the direct visible truth" as if change from physical to spiritual is an identity with change from particle to wave or vise versa! It actually is! Transference from physical to perceptual is a transformation from world to self, so that it is a transformation or inversion! To say it in correct psychoanalytic terms, a projection becomes an introjection by inversion of position of perception. If this inversion is not perceived, the parties are not talking with each other but past each other. These physical transformations of "particle" to "wave" are appreciated not only by recognition of the unconscious associations, but also, can be detected by spectrophotometer. The author is not fully aware of the capacities and limitations of present spectroscopy. Now (1-26-06), the author is aware of its existence and finds in **Physics** by Zitzewitz (1995)[43] that it is generally used to detect mass by relating mass to wavelength. The corollary of that or the association of that phenomenon with the inverse relationship of mass with frequency of electromagnetic radiation has apparently not been in the "collective consciousness" of the physicists. On this date (1-26-06), it appears, to this author, that the neutrino is energy or "anti-matter" believed to be matter because of mass spectroscopy interpretation. The wave of energy is perceived as the particle of mass. Wave and particle may be inverted as to perception, because of interpretation of spectroscopy data. Zitzewitz's **Physics**[44] relates spectroscopy to wavelength detection and relates detection of matter type by emission spectrum for elements like hydrogen and helium[45].

To change relative positions of masses by motion is to force change of related electrons and protons and electromotive waves or charged particle positions (distances as in d2). "For every action, there is an equal and opposite reaction"(Newton's Third Law). A visible man (or woman) pushes a mass across a platform. The force necessary to move the mass, minus the resistance of friction, generates an electromagnetic wave due to motion of one group of atoms relative to others, because of related mass to charge positions. The different mass to charge ratios gives electron waves more flexibility than proton particles or the center of mass. But notice how the electron wave character greatly changes the center of charge of the mass due to collection of negativity towards the rear of the moving "particle", especially at very high velocity approaching c, the speed of light or electromagnetic waves. Thus the "mutual atomic-molecular polarity" (MAMP) results from different mass/charge ratios and wave/particle "states" of electrons and protons and different center of charge than center of mass. This is just a more clear "identification" of atomic function "apart from the direct visible truth". Yet it is a truthful "identification" consistent with the available information. It is important to recognize that magnetic waves of neutral moving bodies occur at a constant rate at equilibrium but are generated at a more rapid rate during motion. Electromagnetic waves relate directly or inversely to acceleration and deceleration, respectively. It is the forces of acceleration and deceleration or motion relative to other masses that cause the changes in "mutual atomic-molecular polarity". The force of change in this polarity is perceived as inertia. "Uniform linear motion" along the surface of the earth is actually motion along the curved surface of the earth and is not towards or away from the earth's center of gravity. But, the magnetic force of gravity is the Maxwellian force or Coulomb's force caused by the relative motion of two "mutually charged" "particle" "masses" and is a force related, directly to velocity and mass-charge products and, inversely, to separating distance squared. So, acceleration and deceleration forces do not operate on Einstein's railway passenger while he smoothly rides along in the railway car (except during change of direction of motion or change of separating distance). The motion maintains a constant distance from the earth's center of gravity (charge) except during relative change of position, like going up a hill. Change in direction of the railway car on the earth's surface is a change in the electromotive force direction of motion and is therefore an inertial force, not a gravitational one. It is actually a dis-relationship or un-relationship. Use of the word "relativity" in such a change is evidence of disorientation as to true relationships. The perceived force on the passenger in a turn conveys perception of a negative or dissociative relationship of the train's motion to its prior relationship with the earth's surface. This is a well-known phenomenon used in inertial navigation systems. The force on the railway passenger, or on the inertial navigation system, proves change of state of motion by exhibiting lack of relativity! It relates to the consciousness, by acceleration-deceleration forces that indicate perceptual, change of direction of motion as negatively related to the previous state of motion. Professor Einstein's "unified field theory" holds in the atomic model, because uniform circular motion in the atom is centripetal acceleration towards the nucleus caused by charge, as described by Newton for planets etc. with the force of gravity, which we now should see is due to charge-related magnetism. Professor Einstein's paper, relating the electrodynamics of moving bodies[46], uses the magnet-metal rod or wire model in his thoughts rather than neutral masses. "Gravity" is the force of attraction of two mutually related physical bodies that are "neutral in charge". The "logic of relations"[47] "identifies" that force as related to mutual electron and proton charges with associated different masses and mass/charge ratios so that use of a charged rod or wire is acceptable and: $KGFM1 \ M2/d^2 = F = Ccoulomb's \ Fq1q2/d^2$

This is a mathematical "identity" proof of unity. It is an associative, not dissociative, relationship. Since relationships of charged particles are established as related by force, inversely as to distance squared and inviolately present, failure to accept the conceptualization of "MAMP" as truth would exhibit duplicity. It would also seem to be in ignorance of the findings of Maxwell, Coulomb, and Lorentz. This is actually believed by this author to result from the "collective unconscious" of the relatively small forces of "MAMP". Mass to charge and charge to mass ratios are now constant "identities" for "neutral" masses in motion relative to other masses. To label the "equivalent charge" of a "neutral mass" with a symbol: Dc is the constant used to obtain the "equivalent charge", due to "neutral mass" of a "neutral mass" (8.61646 X 10-^{11}Coulombs/kilogram). Since neutral mass and charge are directly related, neutral mass and charge are related to each other by these constants. The complement of centripetal force is centrifugal force and is the "negative force" leading away from unity or increasing the d in the gravity and Coulomb equations. It is electromotive force or inertia. This author's conceptualization of an EAD as a positively charged "particle" that generates electro-magnetic force waves of gravity (or gravitational field of Einstein) and inertia (electromotive force wave or field) can be seen on P. 544, in diagram 26-5 C of Physics by Zitzewitz et. Al (1995)[48]. Since this "particle",EAD, acts upon waves, as if wave, and particles (charges) as if "particles" (charge), it, though one entity, has duplicity of presence. This explains the duality of electro-magnetic "particles". They are both electric charges and magnetic particles, with perception dependent upon position relative to, or dissociative from, the "particle's" motion. The "MAMP" mental model of acceleration and motion of "masses" is a mental model of atomic-molecules as capacitors (charged particles or polar molecules). The acceleration-deceleration of an atomic-molecular "mass" (capacitor) generates an electromotive force, inertia. The uniform motion of an atomic-molecular "mass" (capacitor) generates a magnetic wave, gravity. The waves (electromotive and magnetic) relate to "mass" acceleration (or deceleration) and motion as predicted by James Clerk Maxwell[49]. Maxwell found that changing an electric field's (of electron-proton charges) position causes the magnetic field (of gravity) and changing of the magnetic field (by acceleration or deceleration of motion) causes the electric field. (This is from Zitzewitz P. 544). The parentheses of the previous sentence are the author's). Thus gravity is not a "deformation of space". Gravity is a magnetic field due to motion of a polar or magnetic "mass" and inertia is an electromotive force due to acceleration or deceleration of a polar or magnetically-charged "neutral mass". Failure to accept this model would suggest denial of the "valence bands" and "conductor bands" of atomicmolecules and polarity of molecules in motion. The magnetic force of gravity is similar to the A.) Coulomb forces[50] on

65

charged particles; B.) The magnetic field of gravity results from charges q1 and q2 moving relative to each other (such as Earth and Sun) as related above by Maxwell's generation of a field by motion of charged particles and generation of a force related to that field. Let's check this model with the Third Right Hand Rule of electricity:

1. Recognize that the earth revolves around the sun in a counterclockwise direction[51]. (Baker, Robert H. (1963-64). Astronomy 8th. Ed (P. 18). D. Van Nostrand Co., Inc. Princeton, N.J.).

2. The earth has an "effective positive charge" because EADs are positive charges and the solution of the unity equation of Coulombs force and the Gravity force equations gives: charge equal to $+8.61646 \times 10^{-11}$Coulombs/kg.

3. "The Third Right Hand Rule" is found in **Physics**[52] (p. 502). "The direction of force on a current carrying wire in a magnetic field can be found by using the third right hand rule,": (The earth's north pole is actually its south magnetic pole, Zitzewitz P. 492, because the north pole of the magnet points to it). (a) "Point the fingers of your right hand in the direction of the magnetic field" (Your hand should be held out in the hand shaking position, so that fingers curl towards you). (b) "Point your thumb in the direction of conventional (positive) current flow" of the Earth's revolution about the sun (You are in the sun's position. The earth is your hand. Your thumb points to your left, because the positively charged earth is moving counterclockwise.) (c) "The palm of your hand then faces the direction of the force acting on" the earth by the sun and the sun by the earth. This is gravity. The constant Dc is 8.61646×10^{-11} Coulombs per kilogram for both the masses, sun and earth. The real cause of gravity is the Coulomb force resulting from "Mutual Atomic-Molecular Polarity" as it relates to force in the manner predicted by Maxwell, once it is recognized "neutral mass" has "equivalent charge" or is dipolar in motion.

First Presentation of Einstein's Denial of Force Einstein (1905)[53], in his development of "relativity" and his criticism of Maxwell's electromagnetic theory "as applied to the reciprocal action of a magnet and a conductor", found the Maxwell equations different depending on which mass is "at rest" and which is "moving", yet felt the results must be the same for observers "in any inertial frame of reference". What Einstein failed to recognize due to this "feeling" is that the force applied to masses to accelerate them to motion causes a change in the inertia of those masses (electromotive force) and the "body put into motion" relative to the "body at rest" is not in the same inertial (electromotive force) state. Due to acceleration required to cause motion, the relative electron-proton distance or relationship is changed, due to the limits of c (a real phenomenon found by Einstein). Of course, Einstein did not explain inertia as the electromotive force of acceleration-deceleration to motion of "mass" as relates to charge in the capacitor atommolecules. Further, the relationship of earth to sun is not electromotive or inertial, but is magnetic. Physics is both a qualitative and quantitative thought process. Without specification of the real mass quantities of the magnet and conductor and the direction of motion relative to a defined reference position, Einstein's "thought experiment" of "relativity" is disoriented as to accelerating-decelerating force, direction, and quantity. This suggests "indeterminacy" or disorientation in thought as to perception of demonstrable reality. **Quantities** for direction, relative to some defined origin; for force, relative to some determined mass; and for specific magnet strength and mass and conductor resistance; as well as outside force to the conductor and magnet; need to be specified for any real situation of physical reality to be adequately delineated. Those who will accept Einstein's "relativity" of unequal and moving quantities seem unaware of these real potential differences and their relationships to inertia, force, distance, time, and velocity. It may be Einstein's "charming and engaging" personality that leads us to follow his "relativity", rather than its truthfulness to a reality demonstrable in fact. Einstein's perception that objects are shortened in length as their velocity approaches c, the velocity of light, seems correct and related to his demonstration of light's natural limit of velocity. His observation that perceived mass increases as it is accelerated faster relates to the increasing electromotive resistance of acceleration, while mass actually decreases to EADs of electromagnetic radiation, becoming all energy at c, his limiting velocity of all matter. No one should leave this chapter and believe four dimensions are required to describe real physical phenomena that do occur over time, but relate, directly or indirectly, to specific, determinable times and real locations of different inertial states due to different mass-relationship distances or positions. The primary cause of Professor Einstein's need for four dimensions was his errant determination of the light "particle", as a photon wave one second long. A second cause was the assumption of inertial equivalence, a state provably untrue by inertia's different relationships to different masses. His compensation for these misperceptions with mathematical "transformations" is a character trait he had throughout his career. This consistency of "defensive structure" is typical of a personality functioning very effectively in an untruthful way. Practice makes near perfect.

Einstein's character was inconsistent in that he labeled some, who would not see his atomic model, as having a "positivistic philosophical attitude" that allowed them to believe that if they had all of the facts they could reach a synthesis, while he could not assume a direction and synthesis he had proven. This was a devalued self. Yet, at the same time, he maintained he had a right to "free conceptual construction" to try to reach synthesis of reality without the conception's being required to be related to reality. This was a grandiose self. Einstein was captured in a "split" of self that has captivated many of us. That "split" self appears to relate to a feeling of "knowing" or definition of self by "feeling" rather than reality.

Denials: (1) The Special Theory of Relativity[54] is a denial of absolute time due to denial of the negative relationship of motion to two different positions at the same time (notice how this real state results from the very finding of Einstein of the limit of the speed of light). This confirms Professor Einstein's position that his problems related to the relations (or lack of relations) of distance, time, and space. A universe requires times and places in its determination. His universe varied, as to time and place simultaneously, due to lack of a fixed "identity" of the observer. His global view, that there is a "unified field", holds without the transformation equations and is determinate. "Uniform linear motion" on the surface of the earth is the same motion as that of an electron in nuclear orbit, because both are related to the center of their orbits by centripetal deceleration and centrifugal acceleration. There is "equilibrium" of accelerating and decelerating motions or forces, which relate to electrical forces by obvious charge differences (of protons and electrons) or "mutual atomic-molecular polarity" (of "neutral masses"). The problem of "indeterminacy" for Einstein and quantum mechanics results from calling a "wave", the photon or one second of electromagnetic energy, a "particle" and conceptualizing it as such with the name "photon".[55,56,57] Because a wave has three dimensions, adding a fourth dimension, time, to it is to impute time into its character twice. This is the equivalent of spatial disorientation or inability to determine position due to use of two different times or indeterminate time. Einstein's tolerance of indeterminate time causes indeterminacy. Indeterminate time can be corrected with spatially related or inertially corrected clocks. Use of a true particle of light, the EAD that has only two directions of motion-vibration, with time as the third dimension or space of propagation, grants determination or determinate time and denies indeterminacy or the "Heisenberg uncertainty principle". Since there is no change in energy for an electron in constant orbit, the "Heisenberg's uncertainty principle"[55,56,57] when expressed as change in momentum or energy over time, is improper, because there is no change. Yet, if a change in energy for an electron orbit occurs, it must be precisely h (Planck's constant) or a numerical multiple of it related directly to it, a determinant factor. Therefore, there is no "indeterminacy". This author has come to relate these "energies" or "energy levels" to power and time and the energy of h over time ($1/f$ x one second). These are experimentally determined facts. Planck's constant is actually energy per Hertz or frequency. Since the frequencies have time associated with them, it appears to this author that the photon is the energy required to keep the electron at the higher "energy" level for one second. The EAD is then the energy necessary to keep the electron in the higher orbit for one second divided by the frequency. The fact that a uniform amount of power is required to maintain an electron's position farther from the nucleus, suggests a field force directed towards the nucleus or a common force towards unity of matter, mass, and material thought. This real unifying force or unity force is named, by some, as "God". The potential and kinetic energies of an electron in orbit are equal and constant at the "equilibrium" state of an orbit or shell. Change of orbit or shell is a "transformation" of nature and does not require "transformation equations". The change of orbit to a lower orbit or shell causes loss of mass for the molecule with gain of energy for the EAD (when an EAD, or photon wave of EADs, escapes the atom) and loss of mass for the molecule with lower shell energy level for the electron. It is only when the electron escapes that the electron gains energy, because

69

the gain of energy to the electron wave is gain of mass for the entire molecular "wave". If uncertainty is related to the direction of motion of EAD energy from the atom, the direction is always negative or away from the central nucleus and unity of matter and is perpendicular to the tangent of electron motion at the time of exit. So we are left with the: "Einstein Certainty Principle"

(2) The General Theory of Relativity[58], that starts with the assumption that "all Gaussian coordinate systems are equivalent for the general laws of nature", should be recognized as the mathematical equivalent of a disorientation as to place and time, because it denies a single fixed reference for time and position orientation for all observers. Medically, this is equivalent to disorientation where the patient does not know where in the universe he (she) is or what time it is. Use of "transformation equations" moves the graph, from what should be called "imaginary" numbers, to a functional "real" result. But, transformation equations are a mathematical solution to a cognitive (thought) or perceptual problem. It is equivalent to "operating on" the ego when the superego is the origin of the problem. Use of the "photon" as a "particle", when it is actually a wave, leads to uncertainty. But, Professor Einstein's conceptualization of a "particle" of light was a perception, "apart from a direct visible truth" of a real, naturally occurring entity, now truthfully identified and named the EAD. The EAD, properly "identified", and the finding of "mutual atomic-molecular polarity" leads to the "unified field" where atomic, gravitational, and electromagnetic theories can be seen as one, all electromagnetic, and related to charge or charge-induced wave interactions (particles and/or waves).

(3) Denial of Force: (2-12-06). While Newton's force of gravity and Coulomb's force, due to charge properties, work very well to describe elliptical paths of matter in orbits for the atoms and planets, especially when changes of energy due to loss of sunlight are considered, Einstein describes gravity as a "deformation of space", as if space is an "ether", proven to be non-existent by Michelson and Morley! Einstein denies that gravity is a force, and while everyone else knows space cannot be deformed because it is empty, Einstein suggests it is a rubber blanket or some other "cloth"-like material (proven non-existent) that can be "deformed"! Einstein appears to have a "compulsion to associate" negativity to reality or have a "false transference", misalliance, or

confusion of un-relatedness to "relativity". Gravity is a force! Gravity is the force of electro-magnetism conveyed at the speed of light by magnetic waves perpendicular to the path of earth's motion (relative to the sun or other masses) and towards centers of mass-charge for all bodies. Inertia is the electro-motive force resulting from acceleration-deceleration of charged, polar particles or "masses".

Einstein's Denial of Charge for "Neutral Masses" and Light results from his emptiness as to the charged-particle nature of energy. How is energy explained without mass or charged particles? When force is denied, energy or the product of 1/2Mass X v^2 is lost because force is the cause of velocity. A denial of force as the cause of energy, EAD production as well as motion, leads to denial of force as a product of energy. Denial of force as a product of energy, leads to a "deformation of space" or mysticism. This author cannot accept "deformation of space" as an adequate description of the physical reality of gravity and suggests that description is denial of a real physical force.

For completeness, the three confirmatory "proofs" of Einstein's General Theory of Relativity should be reviewed as to perception using the "Unified Field Theory of 'Charged Particle' Relations and Mass-Energy Transformation". It can be stated as: "All matter and energy of a defined universe are related by charges and their positions in time and space. A change of position of any charge affects all other charges. Electromagnetic force waves are generated by a change of the relative positions of charged particles. Charged particles have different charge/mass ratios. The "EAD" is the single "particle" of electromagnetic energy with energy, h, with a very weak positive charge of EADc, $+1.602 \times 10^{-19}$ Coulombs, mass of EADm 7.372419×10^{-51} kilograms (Kd, copyrighted 03-05-05), and the speed of light. Velocity is positive (+) towards a particular named or designated mass and negative away from it. Energy can be transformed into mass by accelerating charged electrons relative to charged protons of an atom or molecule with loss of the energy of the EADs. This is the "equivalent" of attracting an electron away from a positively charged nucleus. This gain in "mass" results in a loss of the electromagnetic energy from the surrounding space (notice the conservation of mass-energy). Force times distance can be transformed to mechanical and electromagnetic energies during accelerations or decelerations of bodies that are "neutral at rest" and in uniform, "linear" motion. Uniform linear motion differs from uniform circular motion due to inequalities relative to centers of mass of positive and negative accelerating and decelerating forces relative to other masses. Note well that positive force towards deceleration relative to other masses relates the two masses or entity states by electromotive force or inertia or charge from "mutual atomicmolecular polarity" ("MAMP"), but uniform motion affects other masses by magnetic force. Motion away is disassociative, decreasing force, unrelating, not relative. Mass X c^2, energy, and charge in motion at c are equivalents as to quantitative value. Mass and energy are opposite as to sign.

1. The shift of light frequency towards red band from very dense stars is a real observed phenomenon. It is explained by the "Unified Field Theory of 'Charged Particle' Relations and Mass-Energy Transformation" by a shift to mass from energy resulting from a decreased distance of separation of the center of mass of the generating star from the generated light energy. This results in less EAD loss from the denser stars and subsequent shift of light frequency to the red bands (longer wave lengths). This is consistent with mass loss for the escaping light waves, while charge or particle loss is either present or absent for each particle of light. Said differently, each particle of light escapes or does not escape the dense star. The mass-loss to the generated-energy-wave is inversely proportional to the distance squared between dense star and mass of light energy generated. So that, as the distance is shortened or the attractive force increased, fewer EADs escape and the frequency is lessened and the wavelength lengthened towards the red band.

2. Deflection of light passing by the sun from foreign stars visible in an eclipse, results from the "gravitational" or "equivalent gravitational" force of two mutually "charged" bodies or bodies of something directly related to "equivalent" "mass". The equivalence allows "transformation" of "identities". The sun's gravity attracts the "equivalent mass", "charge", or energy by the above-recognized phenomenon of gravity, which is relevant to mass, charge, or energy! Deflection of light in its passage by the sun in eclipse is generally felt to result from the wave nature of light. Light does generate a magnetic wave due to its being a positive charge in motion (EAD). The magnetic wave is gravity. The wave of its

propagation is electric and unidirectional for a single EAD. The stars seem to be farther from the sun's center because their incident rays to earth have been bent by gravity so that their projection back towards origin causes them to be perceived as farther from the sun's center by "projection" of the incident ray to a position different from its origin. The above explanation of movement of the apparent positions of stars as relates to gravity is sufficient to meet the qualitative descriptions generally presented in discussions of this phenomenon. However, in at least one place, Einstein is known to have said this is double what would be expected from Newton's gravity. To meet the "double" challenge, this author points out that the "charged particle" model has both electromotive and magnetic forces and that the electromotive (inertial) forces will be greater on incidence to and exit from the sun's "gravitational field" and equal to gravitational force (magnetic).

3. The "Unified Field Theory of 'Charged Particle' Relations and Mass-Energy Transformation" explains Mercury's forty-three seconds of arc advancement in perihelion. Because mercury is closer to the sun than the other planets, it receives more energy per surface area than they do. This added energy is added "mass" or "charge" which increases gravity of mercury to the sun and centrifugal force away from it. But, the sun is losing significantly more "mass", energy, or "charge" than mercury is gaining, so mercury's orbit is slowly getting larger by 43 seconds of arc angle per year. For our solar system, this is probably true of all the planets, but at a slower rate. The more relevant factor is the distance of separation of the planets from the sun which makes the energy transfers from the SunMercury product (actually mass or mass-energy losses) less and less important with distance of the planets from the sun, because the forces, while related to the equivalent masses, energy, or mutual atomic-molecular polarities, are inversely related to the square of the separating distances.

Finally, to address the "indeterminacy" issues of the Fifth Solvay Congress of 1927[59], which relate to the inability to decide whether to use "wave" or "particle" in talking about electrons and photons: The answer at that time was "indeterminant". Truthful answers as perceived by this author are: (1) Discover that a photon is not a particle but a "bundle" of particles or a wave of particles one second long. (2) Recognize that photon or "bundle" as a wave. (3) When describing the mass of one atom or molecule as resulting from the addition of energy to its electrons' waves, use the wave theory because of the transformation from energy to mass and the wave nature of mass as opposed to particle. Recognize that the net energy of an electron in a stable orbit is zero. (4) When describing electron relationships, recognize complementary duality of charge (particle), spin, and mass (wave) position.

(5) When describing one "EAD" use the "particle" theory. (6) When describing two paired electrons, use the "particle" theory if they are in the same wave and the wave theory, if they are in different waves. (7) When using photons, use the wave theory, because they are in uniform motion and are a wave of EAD "particles". (Apologies: This appears to be the work of a dictator. But, these directions are mandated by the definitions of "wave" and "particle" and the "logic of relations" of these entities as found in nature).

What is the usefulness of this unified field? First, it affirms Albert Einstein's global intuition that a "unified field" exists. Second, it demonstrates unity of the functional character of the universe. Third, it correlates unity of human thought with the function of the universe as electromagnetic. Fourth, it suggests the universe, as we know it, is a unified, non-random, functioning entity with real determinate direction with positive towards mass, matter, or unity. Not so clearly, it suggests fusion by deceleration of electrons and unity of protons can be used to "create" desirable quantities of energy in predetermined quantities under controlled conditions and gives some insights as to technical considerations. The obvious corollary of the production of energy by fusion is the synthesis of complex elements using physical laws and techniques with predictable results. The long sought synthesis of gold from less valuable elements would be a physical feat, not a chemical one. Of note is that Einstein's perceptual reality relative to mass was that it increased with velocity. This author's perception is that mass decreases with velocity due to decreased electron proton-nucleus distance, mandated by the limiting velocity of c, recognized by Einstein. The cause of increasing resistance to motion is increasing production of electromotive force and electromagnetic waves. At c all matter (mass) becomes EADs. The author's perception is that electromagnetic radiation results from the motion of masses, due to decreased electron-proton distance resulting from the limits of c. The limit of c (the velocity of light) is an Einstein finding of fact. Since Einstein's theories are "mirrors" of the present one, as to "wave-particle" and "charged-not charged", his proofs are actually proofs of the "Unified Field Theory of 'Charged Particle' Relations and Mass-Energy Transformation", when the use of "transformation equations" is deleted. "Transformation Equations" are replaced with simpler "Unity Equations" descriptive of, and unity perception of self with, the real natural phenomena.

Einstein's transformation of physics from the mathematical description of real physical phenomena as "happenings" in three dimensional space to an "existence" in the four dimensional world is denial of the reality of the "here and now" or a denial of real time, space, force, mass, inertia, and position. There is no doubt that time changes relationships by the functions of those relationships. But, because of those relationships, all times, positions, and states are not equal. Force does cause changes in mass. Inertia relates to mass (as a quantified particle). Gravity relates to mass (as a wave producing body of specific quantity in motion at specific velocity). Denial of different inertial states of position is denial of unequal mass sizes. Denial of Maxwell's findings is denial of true and "relevant" material. Denial of force is denial of a fundamental concept of physics and a real, bedrock, conceptualization of real natural phenomena. Einstein's "transformation" of the perceptual reality of physics is a testament to his real character and that of his followers, not a true description of real, physical phenomena. His failure to correctly determine the true quantitative character of a "particle" of light and his denial of inertial changes with massive magnet movements, as opposed to light wire movements, denied himself the "unified field". These are "over-idealization –devaluation" characteristics of his personality and are unrelated to his genetic intelligence. He did give us the limit of the speed of light and focused our consciousness on physics and light's part in it. He did not discover the "particle" of light or unit value of electromagnetic energy. The mathematically discovered unit of light, or electromagnetic energy, charge, equivalent mass, and velocity with direction is the EAD, the unit value of the "Unified Field of 'Charged Particle' Relations and Mass-Energy Transformation". The author sincerely hopes the reader will find that the spirit and soul of Professor Albert Einstein have been truthfully presented.

References to Chapter IV:

1 Clark, Ronald (1971, 1984), EINSTEIN – The Life and Times (P.284-289). Avon Books, An Imprint of Harper and Collins Publishers, 10 East 53rdStreet, N.Y., N.Y.

2 Ibid (1) Pp. 251-271.

3 Ibid (1).

4 Ibid (1), P. 504.

5 Ibid (1), P.37.

6 Dostoyevsky, Fyodor (1866). Crime and Punishment.

7 Ibid (1), P. 504.

8 Ibid (1), P. 77.

9 Ibid. (1) P. 118.

10 Weisskopf. "Single Proton Theoretical Rate". Source, The New Encyclopedia Britannica, 15th Edition (1992), Vol. 14: P.377. McHenry, Robert, General Editor; Chicago.

11 Zitzewitz, Paul W. Neff, Robert F. Davids, Mark (1995). Merrill **Physics** Principles and Problems P. 577. Glencoe/Mcgraw-Hill N.Y., N.Y. 12 Ibid (1), P. 493.

13 Ibid (1) P.495.

14 Ibid (1).

15 Ibid (1) P. 33.

16 Kohut, Heinz (1977). "The Restoration of the Self", P.173n. International Universities Press, Inc. N.Y.

17 Ibid (1), P. 133.

18 Ferenzi, Sandor (1932). "Confusion of Tongues Between Adults and the Child". Paper presented at the International Psychoanalytic Congress, September 1932, in Wiesbaden. IJP, 1949. Translation in Masson's ASSAULT ON TRUTH below, Pp. 291-302.

19 Ibid (16).

20 Ibid (11), Pp. 556-560, 712.

21 Ibid (11). All constants in this book are based on data obtained from Merrill **Physics** Principles and Problems by Zitzewitz ET. al.

22 Maxwell, James Clerk (1873). "Treatise on Electricity and Magnetism", as presented by Zitzewitz et al Pp. 542-547.

23 Ibid (11), Pp. 561-564.

24 Ibid (11), Pp. 542-547.

25 Ibid (11) Pp. 415-420.

26 Ibid (1) P. 253.

27 Mc Henry, Robert, General Editor. "The New Encyclopedia Britannica" (1992), 15th 16, Chicago.

28 Kohut, Heinz (1968). "The Psychoanalytic Treatment of Narcissistic Personality Disorders – Outline of a Systematic Approach". Psychoanalytic Study of the Child Vol. 23: Pp. 86-113.

29 Ibid (11), P556-560.

30 Ibid (11) Pp. 561-564.

31 Ibid (11), Pp. 556-560.

32 Masson, Jeffrey M. (1984, 1985). **THE ASSAULT ON TRUTH–** Freud's Suppression of the Seduction Theory Pp. 133. Penguin Books, Viking Penguin, Inc. 40 West 23rd Street, N.Y., N.Y.

33 Kuhn, Thomas S. (1962, 1970, 1996). **The Structure of Scientific Revolutions**, Third Edition. P.5. University of Chicago Press, Chicago, Illinois, 60637.

34 Bion, W. (1967). Second Thoughts: Selected Papers on Psychoanalysis. London: Heinemann, Pp. 86-109.

35 Piaget, Jean (1937), "Principle Factors Determining Intellectual Evolution From Childhood to Adult Life", from Rapaport, David (1951, 1956, 1959), ORGANIZATION AND PATHOLOGY OF THOUGHT: Selected Sources, Pp. 154-192. Columbia University Press, N.Y. Also from: Factors Determining Human Behavior: Harvard Tercentenary Conference of Arts and Sciences, by Edgar Douglas Adrain, et al., Cambridge Mass.: Harvard University Press, Copyright 1937 by the President and Fellows of Harvard College.

36 Ferenzi, Sandor (1932). **Confusion of Tongues Between Adults and the Child**. Paper presented at the International Psychoanalytic Congress, September 1932, in Wiesbaden. IJP, 1949. Translation in Masson's THE ASSAULT ON TRUTH below, Pp. 291-302.

37 Ibid (34).

38 Ibid (32).

39 Einstein, Albert (1905). "On A Heuristic Point of View Concerning the Production and Transformation of Light." Annalen der Physik 17: 132-148, from the Collected Papers of Albert Einstein V. 2 86-103. Princeton University Press, 41 William Street, Princeton, N.J., 08540.

40 Ibid (11), Pp. 546,576, 578.

41 Ibid (11), 542-547.

42 Ibid (11), P. 415-420.

43 Ibid (11), Pp. 546, 576-578.

44 Ibid (11), P. 576.

45 Ibid (11), P. 578.

46 Einstein, Albert (1905). "On the Electrodynamics of Moving Bodies". Annalen der Physik 17: 891-921. Also found in the Collected Papers of Albert Einstein Vol. 2: Pp. 140-171. Princeton University Press, 41 William Street, Princeton, N.J., 08540.

47 Ibid (35).

48 Ibid (11), P.544.

49 Op. Cite.

50 Ibid (25).

51 Baker, Robert H. (1963-64). Astronomy 8th. Ed. (P. 18). D. Van Nostrand Co., Inc. Princeton, N.J.

52 Ibid (11), P. 502.

53 Ibid (46).

54 Einstein, Albert (1961). "The Special Theory of Relativity". **Relativity**: The Special and General Theory, Pp. 3-64. Three Rivers Press, N.Y., N.Y. 55 Pauling, Linus (1935, 1963). Introduction to **Quantum Mechanics Quantum Mechanics** 436). General Publishing Company, Ltd. 30 Lesmill Road, Don Mills, Toronto, Ontario, Canada.

56 Miller, Franklin (1959). **College Physics** Pp. 506-508. Harcourt, Brace, and World, Inc. N.Y.

57 Zitzewitz, Paul W.; Neff, Robert F. (1990, 1992, 1995). Merrill **Physics**: Principles and Problems, P. 568. Glencoe/McGraw Hill, 936 Eastwind Drive, Westerville, Ohio, 43081.

58 Einstein, Albert (1961). "The General Theory of Relativity". **Relativity**: The Special and General Theory, Pp.67-116. Three Rivers Press, N.Y., N.Y. 59 Ibid (1), Pp. 416-419.

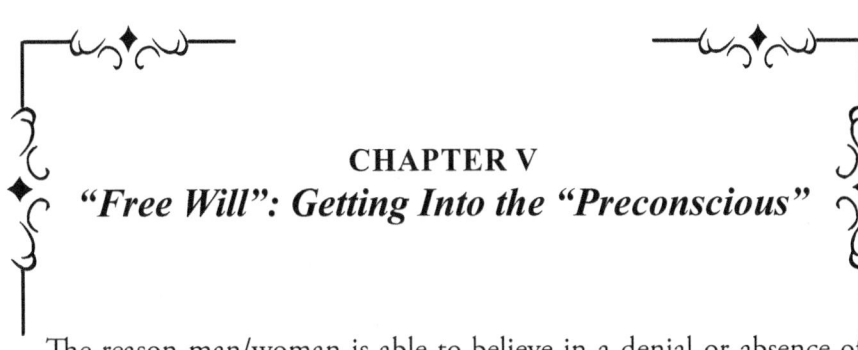

CHAPTER V
"Free Will": Getting Into the "Preconscious"

The reason man/woman is able to believe in a denial or absence of absolute truth is because of man's/woman's "free will" to choose an exclusive association of "self" with positive or negative reality and the resulting "split" of consciousness that the exclusive association of "self" with either of those states as exclusive realities gives. This statement's truthfulness, as determined by its' provable real functions, verifies the reality of "free will". The process of choosing an alliance of "self" with a position should be recognized to occur in the "preconscious" state of mind and is the "identifier" of the "core" of one's personality, value system, or superego. The psychoanalysts' exclusive association of themselves with "knowing" reality as a "principle" denies them knowledge of the psychical reality of their patients and is the "identifier" of the "core" of their group personality. Their "self" "identification" as "knowing" is the functional process of their preconscious mind and is an exclusive "identification" of themselves as the "normal scientists" with reality or truth, as suggested by Thomas Kuhn. This is an aggressor state of mind of the preconscious that determines their fantasy world as the "fantasy world of brilliance". This narcissistic state is a split state of consciousness where there is one attitude for self and a separate attitude for object. For this reason, its duplicity is obvious. The attitude to self is positive and the attitude to object is negative with neither having absolute truth. In the case of narcissism with the "fantasy world of brilliance", the positive attitude for self is "knowing" and the negative attitude for object is "not knowing". The pivotal point of positive and negative, since it is an assumed non-real state of fantasy, is the "transference" from primary object to later objects, so that all relationships "mirror" the primary relationship with the "child's" projection of "self" as parent (aggressor as to knowing) in later relationships. Albert Einstein's and current physicists' perception of a false identity of the "particle of energy", with no holes between integers and no negative real state (mass), denies them of Einstein's greater consciousness of "The Unified Field". Exclusive association of those "self(ves)" with negative reality is a denial to their consciousness of positive reality and its real functions, including the "identification" of the negative reality of their current perception. Both "Great Men", Freud and Einstein, "identified" themselves with the negative in statements suggesting truth was "unknowable".[1,2] Readers should recognize the duplicity in these "Great Men" of both seeing themselves as "brilliant" or in the know implicitly and suggesting that perceptions that they could not project were "unknowable" or something "we will never know, never". Such a denial of positive identification of all reality can and does result from its' absence in the real early life experiences of many developing personalities who are later found to associate "self" with negative reality and deny positive reality due to their own life experiences as conceptualized by their negative objects (parents, or the untruthful "Great Man" of their "normal science"). The absolute reality of such personalities is that their survival needs have been met in a fashion that has been untruthful to the real emotional (soul) value of their "self". Their real physical survival denies emotional self, but over-idealizes emotional object (when the object is not loving-truthful), due to a "free will" adoption of the fantasy world of real, but negative (untruthful-unloving) emotional object. Physical requirements are met by this "free will" acceptance of physical nourishment in exchange for emotional adoption of the object's emotional perception(s) (the object's world-view, fantasy world, or superego). For this reason, physical requirements are met by "identification with the world view" of the primary object, who may be loving and truthful or not (negative). In the case of the "not" or negative, the "negative transference" is the result. Because of the "split" between the emotional and real (interest) "self" and object (for the negative object), there is no unity of reality of emotional and interest "self" for these persons developing the negative personality. In development of the whole "self" it is important that the manner of the caretaker be loving and shown by truthful action and conceptualization towards the developing child. A "negative transference" as a result of a negative environment is a proof of truthfulness of the phenomenon of "transference" and proof of the reality of "free will". The "split" of "self" is caused by the "free will" exclusive choice of "self association with an untrue reality description (fantasy world or false belief)" that denies truth or positive existence of truth to the perception of those emotionally disoriented to truth. This is the Fantasy world = Parent-child complex. It is actually the child's "self identification" with parental (superego) projection of a false fantasy world as reality (such as the unreal fantasy world states of "brilliance" or "knowing", "unlimited power", or "unlimited wealth"). The negativity or untruthfulness of this fantasy world is no more in the conscious mind of the parent, or "Great Man" of a "normal science", than it is for the "child". It is simply an untrue "defense mechanism" used to attempt to meet the needs of life's circumstances or defend the "self" (of parent or "Great Man") from those needs or circumstances.

Yet, is there really a "free will" choice as to self-association, since the "self" has previously been "split" between the needs of interest and emotional "self", by denial of emotional "self" by real (negative) objects? To the perception of developing negative personalities, the only real choice for survival becomes a "split" between real interest needs for survival and real emotional "self". For them, interest survival requires emotional death. Anatomically, this becomes left hemispherical brain life with right hemispherical brain death. They become "dead", since the right cerebral hemisphere is the hemisphere of "self-image". Does this line of thought allude to Judeo-Christian-Islamic literature? It most certainly correlates with neuroanatomy and neurophysiology!

"Life" of the "self", as an emotionally perceived real "self-image," is then dependent upon and available to only those, who by their own "free will", choose to be aware of the real interest andemotional needs of "self" and "object(s)". This requires a "free will" lack of inhibition of right hemispheric or emotional perception, not a conscious choice for such inhibition! Is this bimodal perception, as an "identification" of "self", available to the unloved child, denied by parents due to other core "interests" and societies with interests defined by those same parents? It is easy to see defective parenting in the societies of our enemies. Is it not more important to see the defects of our own?

The "free will" of bimodal perception of self and object, unity of interest and emotional "self", is a learned skill of avoidance of "identification with the aggressor" mode to find truthful common interests and real emotional bonds. It is a process of "identification" with a truthful and loving parent or "Great Man". "Free will" is a choice of love or hate, and in the negative personalities, has been a choice of love of the negative (untruthful and unloving parent or "Great Man"). Rather than find the negative parent, and his/her fantasy world-view, these personalities see a negative genetic-self and world. To these negative personalities, defects are genetic, not developmental. Problems are negatives of the world, not positive potentials for "self" action. Negative personalities have "false transferences" or false "identifications". The truthful "identification" is the one of "self" with truth and love, both interest and emotion. Has truthfulness been a real "identification" model (mode) for you? Or, is the "identification" that truth is "unknowable" your model (mode)?

The question of "free will" is the question, "Does man/woman have the ability to choose between good and evil, truth and fantasy?" Its' answer is, universally, that he/she does, only if, he or she perceives reality with a truthful model, an "identifier" or "identification" mode or model that is true to reality. A central, "core identity", perception of this book should be that "free will" may not be "real" in all persons because their perceptual reality is changed from truth by truth's false conceptualization. The superego (parents, "Great Men" of Freud and Einstein) has falsely conceptualized true psychoanalytic perceptions of the personality disorders and the "particle of energy" (energy-mass-charge unity element) by the "Oedipal complex" and the "photon". The original "transference" of such a "false alliance" or conceptualization was the conveyance of the mental disorder hysteria by the association of the word "love" with the rape or verbal valuation of children as merely sexual objects. Faulty perception is viewed by defective personalities as genetic (from genes), because their perceptual reality has been developed outside their conscious control by false conceptualization. Their "free will" for physical survival (or survival in their "normal science") develops at the expense of their emotional survival, because of a failure to become aware of the "split" of self and object as to emotional reality by defensive fantasy worlds of "knowing". This is denial of reality by "free will" acceptance by the "child" of a fantasy conceptualization usually presented to children by their parents as the parent's(s') world view, but in the case of a "normal science" as the "world view" of its' "Great Man".

"Free will", when recognized as the ability to choose between good and evil, with perception of good and evil as learned values that might conflict with a real, but untrue core value system, cannot be assumed as "reality" for all persons. It is a true paradox that "free will" is a gift, or taught process, to find truth for the self or the "ideal self". "Free will", as a concept, is an assumption that there is a true ("ideal self") path for best selfinterest, whether the true path is recognized, consciously, or not. When reality is inverted by a false worldview, good becomes evil. When Freud conceptualized reality as his truth for the Oedipal complex, he defined reality as the evil state and when Einstein conceptualized the "photon" as one second of light energy, he defined reality with time and, almost simultaneously, said time was not universal. He also issued a "Confusion of the Tongues" in his concept of a "particle" of energy, defining a "particle" of energy as a wave of energy particles one second long. For all persons to choose right, it is necessary to make clear that what is "right" (true) is best for the fulfillment of their core value system. But to lead a person to truth, when that person's value system is false, requires revelation to that person that his value system (world view), is not truly identifiable with his/her best interest and emotional "self". To do this in one instance may not be difficult. But, to reveal that a person's value system or core value is false, generally as opposed to randomly, is much more difficult. Recognition that an inverted sense of truth, or good and evil, does exist in some people is real and is suggested by the concept of "predestination" and the diagnosis of "psychopathic" or "antisocial" personality(ies). The concept of "predestination" results from the failure to perceive conscience as a result of an environmentally related, "self identification" process and is similar to the psychoanalysts suggesting "personality" might result from genetic factors. For this author, that is failure to separate the genetic person from the personality, conceptually. Failure to recognize perception of good and evil as environmentally related is a state of denial or ignorance of the primary relationship(s). Even superficially, it is easy to see motives for this denial or ignorance. In the case of the child, it has as its motive, a need to believe in a positive (rather than negative) association of self with an object upon whom survival depends. It is this motive that leads to conceptual misalliance or "mesaliance" and inversion of "free will". "Free will" is the concept of the primary relationship as a true conceptualization of reality, so that the child can actually find his/her own "best interest" in the "real world" without disorientation. The requirement of that conceptualization seems to be that the child has, as his/her "ideal self", truthfulness to reality. Without truthful conceptualization of reality in the primary relationship(s), there is no truthful "free will" or "identifier" for the child to "identify" with. Negative persons, therefore, deny the existence of "free will" and see it and absolute truth as unreal or "unknowable". For the Calvinists the motive, to find the conceptualization of "predestination", was similar to that of the psychoanalysts, to say that cure of the antisocial personality is hopeless, in that it is easy to suggest salvation or finding the "true self" for antisocial personalities is impossible for them, and, therefore, does not require any effort. The process of leading a person with a false core value system (world view) to "free will" is, or should be, the art and science of psychoanalysis. Psychoanalysis is, therefore, finding the patient's aggressor identity with a particular fantasy or false belief (transference) and leading the patient to replace the aggressor identity with real object identity (love) and the fantasy world with perceptual truth (reality). This is made difficult when the analyst(s) falsely believe(s) him/herself to hold "truth" without true associations with real events in **patients**' lives and when challenged suggest psychoanalysis is a technique, rather than an art and science. This author presents his associations for the reader to validate or criticize and recognizes growth can occur for him in such an analytic process that focuses upon the validity or false value of his associations as presented and recorded in writing.

This author has been a witness that, "The core of personality, a person's world-view, is formed by primary relationships", but, that most persons perceive their world-views as coming from "self" (ego or id) and not superego (parent or the "Great Man" of their "normal science"). This has been shown, in this book, to be true of practitioners of psychoanalysis as a "normal science" and is also seen to be true of physicists in their perception of their "normal science".

It is hoped the reader will forgive this author's failure to review the extensive literature(s) on personality and "free will" and, therefore, his lack of references. While the dedication part of this book has already been written and suggests that, on the advice of my mother, I will make

84

no further attempts to convince the physicists of the true reality of the "unified field", the following chapters are a record of the attempts to do so by submission of more "papers" to the journal *Nature*. Each chapter is interpreted and paired or "mapped with" the response of the journal. The reader could interpret each "paper" to *Nature* as a psychoanalytic attempt to bring those editors, with a known bias against the "unified field theory", to recognize its' reality as a truthful perception of the physical functioning of our universe.

Predictably, according to Thomas Kuhn, the early verbal and conscious behavior of "normal scientists" to the threat of scientific revolution is not cognizant of past false alliances of "self". Specifically, in the case of the physical scientists (*Nature's* editors), there is as yet no recognition of: 1) The "false alliance" of themselves with an untrue "identification" of the "particle" of energy; 2) Their lack of self association with the phenomenon of energy to mass transformation as an incremental, low temperature, common earthly process at the molecular level; 3) Their lack of self association with energy as "anti-matter" or with the concept that energy should have a mathematical sign (-) opposite that of mass. The following three papers present the elemental unit of mass, energy, and charge as the requisite unifying unity element for perception of the unified field. Currently denied by the physics community are: 1) The EAD as the elemental unit of mass, energy, and charge. 2) That transformation to mass occurs when light energy is captured by a mass so that that energy no longer has the speed of light but increases the atomic-molecular polarity of mass, thereby increasing "mass". 3) That energy is the negative state of matter or $Mc^2 = -E$. The reader might consider that the reason *Nature's* editors will not publish the following papers is because the ego of *Nature's* editors is one of "knowing", instead of finding, "truth". Thus, as for all previous "scientific revolutions", the delay in progress relates to the egocentrism of "knowing". The reader(s) will remember that the perception of the earth as a sphere or "round" was delayed for many years, because "everyone" perceived the earth as "flat". The reason publication is denied is, not because the papers are not "the sort of firm advance in general understanding that would warrant publication in *Nature*", but is, because these papers deny the editors of *Nature* their conscious state of "knowing". The papers must be denied, or negated, to preserve the reality of the fantasy world(s) of brilliance for the editor(s) of *Nature*. The reader, and this author, might reasonably wish to know the identity of the specific editor(s) at *Nature* who made this denial (negative) decision. Sophisticated readers of this book will realize that such editors will be "the last to know" truth because of their firm belief in their own "knowing" state. This is, of course, Albert Einstein's "positivistic philosophic attitude" used to describe those who would not recognize his atomic model as true.

Let us now redefine "free will" as a process or "the ability to choose between good and evil that results from consciously looking for association of self in our mental conceptualization of relationships with truthfulness, whether those relationships relate to natural phenomena or other persons". This then determines that our preconscious process of perception become conscious and truthful to the real state of things, whether positive or negative in its relation to self-interest. In this manner, or by this process, there is an emotional (spiritual, right cerebral hemispheric self) alliance with truthfulness that makes the "self" allied with the real world or in unity with it. With "negative free will", or denial of conscious alliance of "self" with truthfulness, there is a loss of ability to choose between good (truth) and evil (fantasy), because of loss of the relationship of "self" to truth. There is, therefore, a death of true self. This author presents as truth that *Nature's* denial of his papers is a "death" of the true self of *Nature* due to editor'(s)' untruthful denial(s), as expressed by the response that these papers do not present "the sort of firm advance in general understanding that would warrant publication in *Nature*".

The reader might consider that the reason *Nature's* editor(s) will not publish the following papers is because the ego of *Nature's* editor(s) is one of "knowing", instead of finding, "truth" (reality). Thus, as for all previous "scientific revolutions", the delay in progress relates to the egocentrism of "knowing", an unreal state for them in their conceptualization of the "unified field" of our one universe as a negative reality. The reason publication is denied is, not because the papers are not "the sort of firm advance in general understanding that would warrant publication in *Nature*", but is, because these papers deny the editors of *Nature* their conscious state of "knowing". The papers must be denied, or negated by lack of recognition, to preserve the "reality" of the fantasy world(s) of brilliance for the editor(s) of *Nature* or for "normal science" as they know it. What is not consciously recognized by these editors is that they are being evaluated as to truthfulness in their reaction to presentation of new theses that require demonstration as to their process of knowing as opposed to whether they know or not. A "scientific revolution" should now be recognized as a period in which scientists recognize that finding the answer to a problem in their "normal science" results from re-conceptualizing that normal science's world-view so that it describes the world more generally, but at the same time, more truthfully. Sophisticated reader(s) of this book will recognize inability to change one's "world view" due to the intensity and long term use of its fixation, as well as the status acquired in its practice, as the reason why young scientists, or scientists new to the disciplines, usually cause the "scientific revolutions".

As with the psychoanalysts, this author anticipates a likely defensive strategy for the physical "normal scientists" is to state that this author has a "fantasy of brilliance" for himself. This is a specific time that the author wishes to deny "brilliance", defined as "having the ability to know without association of the state of knowing to true facts of reality", as a real or true state for anyone. In this way, the debate becomes the question: "Does the conceptualization, as given, describe reality truthfully?" The reader(s) will see, in the following chapters, that this author has presented to the editor(s) of *Nature* the perceived fact that it is possible to find the unified field with "identification" of its unity element, the EAD, and that this "identification" is either true or not true. But, the editor(s) do not address this "identification", at all, in their responses. While the "identification" of the EAD conceptualization as the unity element for the unified field has nothing to do with "brilliance", its truthfulness as a conceptualization does relate to truth or its absence for that mathematical perception as a true conceptualization of reality. The EAD conceptualization, as a unity element for charge-direction, energy, and mass, either truthfully describes the unity element(s) of the universe and unified field or it does not. That determination requires a conscious look at the EAD conceptualization, as demonstrated by its specific mention, not denial by negation (unconscious denial of its existence), protective of the editor(s) "fantasy world of brilliance". Reader(s) should recognize that the editor(s)' denial of this author's work by "negation" is protection of a "kingdom" or exclusive right-to-know for those editors and exhibits previously described "feelings of entitlement", while their assertion that the decision is made because of they "are unable to conclude that the work provides the sort of firm advance in general understanding that would warrant publication in *Nature*" is viewed as a "defense mechanism" allowing them to avoid addressing the true issue as to whether the thesis is true. It is, for this author, the editor(s) lack of addressing the EAD concept(s) that "identifies" the core of their personality(ies) as the fantasy state of "brilliance". Because this author's positions are not yet coincident with those currently believed to "be in the know", they are not yet the "science" of this age. Because the editor(s) of *Nature* identify self as associated with science, "brilliance", and those "in the know", rather than those seeking truth, they cannot yet publish this author's work.

Most important for the reader(s) of this work is his/her own recognition of how "free will" relates to him/her self and his/her consciousness. Each reader should now recognize that it is the "free will" choice of "self" association with some "world view" that determines the focus of consciousness or the conscious reality of "self". A "free will" association of the reader's "self" with any fantasy-world-view is a denial of that self, person, to consciousness of the broader truthful reality. "Identification" of "self" with any fantasy world "defense mechanism" denies him/her "self" of real life. In regard to the truthful realities presented in this book, failure to identify the self with those truths is not only a disservice to science but is also a disservice to self for the gains self could make by that truthful identification. Since the unified field, as perceptual reality, gives unity of self and self perception(s) with reality, lack of its perception is a separation of self from reality or a death of self. Who would, knowingly, choose death when life is available? Do you believe it is time that truthfulness and denial of absolute "relativity" (positive associations for all reality) be expected of our scientists and, especially, the editors of our scientific journals? Is it time that truthfulness be recognized as the most real value of our "self", just as it is for Washington, Lincoln, and others?

References for Chapter V:

1 Freud, Sigmund. (1938). "**An Outline of Psychoanalysis**". Standard Editions 23: Pp. 141-207, (196).

2 Clark, Ronald (1971, 1984), ***EINSTEIN – The Life and Times***(P. 504). Avon Books, An Imprint of Harper and Collins Publishers, 10 East 53rd Street, N.Y., N.Y.

CHAPTER VI
Mathematical Perception of a Unified Field Theory or Its Loss

Interpretation:

This "paper" was presented to **Nature**4-14-06 as a mathematical analysis as to how the "unified field" had been lost by improper mathematical description of real physical phenomena. Though the problem of the "unified field" is considered the primary problem of physics today, the journal **Nature's** response to this "paper" was to refuse its' publication without recognition of the paper by name or assigned number and without recognition of the reviewer as a person separate from the journal, **Nature**. While readers of this book might not be surprised by the response of **Nature**, this author is surprised each time such an "empty" response is given to a serious attempt to solve a real problem that is apparently not perceived as such by those who are supposed to know or find its' solution and do (have) not! Folks, we are talking about our ability to obtain energy from fusion and other such important and useful basic functions of physical reality. The physicists' position that such things are "unknowable" denies us of that energy, while it gives them the license to do nothing!

Summary-Introduction:

This brief paper is an incomplete presentation of a formidable quantity of work done to solve "The Unified Field" problem presented by Professor Albert Einstein, with mathematical rigor and uncanny perception. It is a mathematical projection of a unified field perception acquired by determination of the field's unit "particle" and recognition of "equivalent charge" as associated with, paradoxically, "neutral mass". It avoids time's "indeterminacy" by using c and avoiding time in equations. "Uncertainty" is eliminated with conscious perception of "transformation(s)". Direction problems, of the atomic and like-charge segments, are solved by the real phenomenon that, in a physical world where electrons are defined to have negative charge, the positive direction is found to be towards unity of matter and charge whether charge is positive or negative, like or unlike. This leads to the finding that perceptual truth is recognition of a positive force towards unity of atoms. Perceptual inversion has been related to dealing with natural transformations with transformation equations and failure to achieve parity perception with nature. This theory does not violate the "Second Law of Thermodynamics", but describes its' direction (randomness) as negative or towards energy from mass. After discovery-developments of the unity element, it is possible to project a true "unified field equation".

Manuscript:

Einstein's geodesic curve, of the "d" of gravity, is a Riemannian summation or a curve of Riemannian geometric perception. A Riemannian summation has definite, fixed lower limits of its' vertical and horizontal "partition" quantities that represent non-curved transformations, rather than transitions, of quantity y over quantity x (distance (position) over time-space or energy-mass over time-space). The time-space continuum is the reality that "c" determines "d"/t. This is a real and true finding of Einstein after Michelson-Morley. To apply the "definite" Riemannian Integral or a continuous function to a Riemannian Summation is to introduce "uncertainty" of magnitude as large as the "partition" in either parameter (x or y, distance or time) as large as the "elementary" or "unit" quantities of reality perception and does not "relate" to reality, but relates a mathematical projection of reality perception. The "indeterminacy" of such a "definite" Riemannian Integral is related to units of measure or perceptual intensity errors as great as c/f for d and $h/(1/f)$ for mass-energy. When f is one, limits are c or ∞(infinity) and h or indeterminacy. At infinity, perception should be considered indeterminate. But, if mass and energy are perceived as conjugal complements, positional reality is determined by c and known directional vector or position of the energy as a "mass-location" of the atom-molecule. The perceptual detail at f = ∞is absolute. It is also absolute for f = 1, when perception of the relative values of all unit qualities and quantities are real and perceived in their true state. For, then, the unit "partitions" are recognized as real and indivisible. It is then recognized that a Riemannian Sum, rather than a "definite" Riemannian Integral, must be used for absolute determinations of transmutation phenomena. Clearly, "definite" Riemannian Integrals can be used, but should not be a cause of loss of reality perception by denial of real partitions due to transformations. "Transformation" of energy-to-mass does occur at the atomic level on earth by electron acceleration to greater mass ("higher energy levels"). Einstein's perception of "d" and "M," of the gravity equation, relates "d" as a function of the effects of mass, M, upon space or "d" as relative to mass(s). The theory presented here suggests F (force) is a function of M (mass radiations of EADS) and "d" (distance) and that F (force) decreases with loss of EAD "particles" to "the greater universe" associated with an increase of "d"(distance). The expression hf over unit-times, a to b, can be expressed as $\int_a^b hf \times dt$. But, this "definite" integral introduces "uncertainty" of magnitude $\subseteq h$ and t equal to $\subseteq$ one second, when h is an indivisible unit quantity or fundamental and elemental property of nature and one second is a defined human projection that could be perceived, incorrectly, as infinitely divisible for the physical phenomena (hf1-n) in question. If there is "indeterminacy" of h relative to time, the perception should be that, "Something other than time is causing the change in h quantity!" The cause is a "transformation" of h energy (EADe) to its equivalent mass EADm (or vice versa). Since the error of the Riemannian "definite" integral is no more than h/hf, for all frequencies (f), it is usually extremely small relative to the quantities of Quantum Electro-Dynamics (QED). That very quantity, h, is definitely certain and relatively large for one or unit (atomic) transformations of energy-mass and could be seen as ∞(infinity). It was actually shown by Einstein, as presented by Pauling (1935)[1], to be the determinate factor as to whether chemical reactions occur. So, the importance of this energy-to-mass transformation (as well as its parity complement, mass-to-energy), and its unit quantity cannot be overemphasized! The quantity, hf, is real and discontinuous, so in "Particle Electro-Dynamics" (PED), hf1-nmust be calculated as a summation and perceived as incremental in reality of process. To do so is to remove uncertainty of energy (equal to hf (f =1/sec.) for all frequencies) by real perception of the (mass or energy) form for each incremental atommolecule and to recognize electromagnetic "transformation(s)", at the atomic level, as ninety-degree parities of energy and mass. This ninety-degree parity is that of Faraday and Maxwell and could be perceived as a "mirage" of the real motion of charged particles (electrons).

92

Mathematically

The unreal "Definite" Riemannian Integral: $\int_a^b$ hf dt, gives "uncertainty", to the Real Riemannian Summation: hf1 + hf2 +... hfn, for all frequencies 1-n, $\subseteq$ h/1 sec. Among other needs, "The Unified Field" perception requires recognition of 6.626 x 10^{-34} Joules as a fundamental or elemental property of one electromagnetic radiation or EAD1. This fundamental property, EADe, or elementary "particle" EAD1, has elemental charge or the unit of charge of quantity equal to + 1.6022 x 10^{-19} Coulomb(s) (EADc, found mathematically by calculating charge at c required to yield 6.626 x 10^{-34} Joules energy), and a mathematically equivalent "mass" of 7.372 x 10^{-51} kg. (EADm found mathematically by M = $^{E/c2}$), at velocity c, with direction positive (+) towards unity of mass. The elementary "particle", EAD1, by What's Your (Analyst's) Diagnosis? Truth (or Fantasy)? transformation(s), gives "The Unified Field Theory of 'Charged Particle' Relations and Mass-Energy Transformation(s)" and its' "Equation".

Reality of perception of this theory requires perception of "equivalent charge" in motion as real or as a real mirror (parity) of an electron's motion (electrons' motions). Clearly, the charges are in parity, have directional quality, and exhibit parity at ninety degrees, rather than 180 degrees (from Maxwell2). "Mass" is perceived as a "wave" quantum. Charge-in-motion or "Equivalent-charge-in- motion" is perceived as a "particle", or particles in a summated wave of unit charges, but is equivalent to unit mass or wave mass as appropriate for EADn, where n is any integer, positive or negative (M or E). The units of mass, energy, and charge are equivalents at c, a "fundamental" v, discovered so by Einstein. "Neutral Mass" has an equivalent charge Dc (calculated mathematically, using equality of gravitational and Coulomb equations of equality of force, to be 8.61646 x 10^{-11} Coulombs/kg.). The implications of this mathematical, reality perception are nearly infinite but result from a very small perception.

"The Unified Field Theory of 'Charged Particle' Relations and Mass-Energy Transformation(s)" "Equation" Can be written:

(For the atom(s)): Δ^{Mc2}= ΔE = EADn x -EADe = EADn x EADm x c^2 = +/-EADn x EADc at velocity c (dependent upon + as towards mass or location in question) = $^{(For\ Gravity):}$ 1/2(G((M1M2/d1^2) + (M1ΔM2Δ/d2^2))) ^{x} Δ^d = (For Electromagnetism): 1/2(K((q1q2/d1^2) + (q1Δq2Δ/d2^2))) x

Δd ^{For Gravity and Electromagnetism} Δd is positive when decreasing. Perception of the EAD1as a "particle" is intuitively apparent when thought of as "mass" or "charge". But when the EAD1is thought of as energy, it is intuitively perceived as a "wave", even though it is only one "particle" of such a commonly perceived wave phenomenon of EADs or EADn. This paper does not directly address the mass-charge or energy changes related to velocity, addressed by Einstein and Heaviside.

Discussion:

This paper suggests, with mathematical rigor, that lack of parity-and-unity perception of real parities of physical phenomena causes "indeterminacy". One such parity is the real and fixed quantity of energy of a single EAD associated with mass and charge (actually two ninety-degree parities associated with electromagnetic phenomena). This paper could continue indefinitely, because it relates to all real physical phenomena, directly or indirectly, and promotes parity perception of reality as physical and psychological equivalence. Inability to recognize the reality of "the Unified Field" results from lack of perceptual intensity, relates to motives of perceptual reality, and is measurable by the "partition" size of a specific "definite" Riemannian Integral. If "partition" size is small enough "to meet the needs of the situation" determinacy is real and is the reason to call the Riemannian Integral "definite". If not, Riemannian Summation or true "logic of relations"3must be used. Lack of parity indicates perceptual inversion. Reality perception of "The Unified Field" results from perception of transmutation or transformation of energy to mass. When "transformation equations" must be used to explain real data, look for perceptual inversion and duplicity of thought. Einstein's "Unified Field" is perceived or lost, dependent upon perception of the real "partition" quantities and/or unity identities of transformation(s) for mass-energy and energy-mass transformation(s). This paper attempts to present physical reality as "a mathematical expression of formal simplicity", (Sir Arthur Eddington)[4]. A new "identification" for physics is the EAD1,e,m,cidentity(ies), and its identity equation segments, for the atomic transformations of mass-energy or energy-mass, gravity-mass-motion mechanics, and electromagnetic-charge-force mechanics. The unifying theory of the universe is that of electromagnetism with the EAD as its' unitary or unifying "particle". This "Unified Field Theory

94

of 'Charged Particle' Relations and MassEnergy Transformation(s)" is an extension of Quantum Electro-Dynamics to Particle Electro-Dynamics of unit transformations. While not discrediting quantum findings, except as to "uncertainty", it explains that "uncertainty" as either a lack of perception or error in its projection.

A more general mathematical finding of this work is that, for equations $y = mx + b$ where b is 0, x can be perceived as an independent variable when it is actually dependent upon m. This is true when y must be an integral multiple of m. In such a case, both y and x are variables dependent upon m and are functions of m in quality and quantity. The specific example given here is $E = hf + 0$, where f is a function of h transformation(s) of energy to mass or mass to energy. The entire paper suggests nonlinear or non-curvilinear interpretations of Planck's findings. Planck's findings suggest a "particle", incremental, discontinuous process of mass-energy or energy-mass transformation(s). Such a process must be described mathematically as a summation, or recognized as nonlinear in product quantity, to avoid "uncertainty" in mathematical projection.

References for Chapter VI:

1 Pauling, Linus; Wilson, E. Bright–Jr. (1935, 1963). *INTRODUCTION TO QUANTUM MECHANICS* With Applications to Chemistry P. 26. Dover Publications, Inc. N.Y.

2 Maxwell, James Clerk (1873). "*Treatise on Electricity and Magnetism*", as presented by Zitzewitz et al Pp. 542-547. Zitzewitz, Paul W. Neff, Robert F. Davids, Mark (1995). Merrill PhysicsPrinciples and Problems P. 577. Glencoe/McGraw-Hill N.Y., N.Y.

3 Piaget, Jean (1937). *Principle Factors Determining Intellectual Evolution From Childhood to Adult Life* is from: Rapaport, David (1951, 1956, 1959), *ORGANIZATION AND PATHOLOGY OF THOUGHT*: Selected Sources, Pp. 154-192. Columbia University Press, N.Y. Also from: Factors Determining Human Behavior: Harvard Tercentenary Conference of Arts and Sciences, by Edgar Douglas Adrain, et al., Cambridge Mass.: Harvard University Press, Copyright 1937 by the President and Fellows of Harvard College.

4 Clark, Ronald (1971, 1984), *EINSTEIN – The Life and Times* (P. 496). Avon Books, An Imprint of Harper and Collins Publishers, 10 East 53rd Street, N.Y., N.Y. FED 04-13-06.

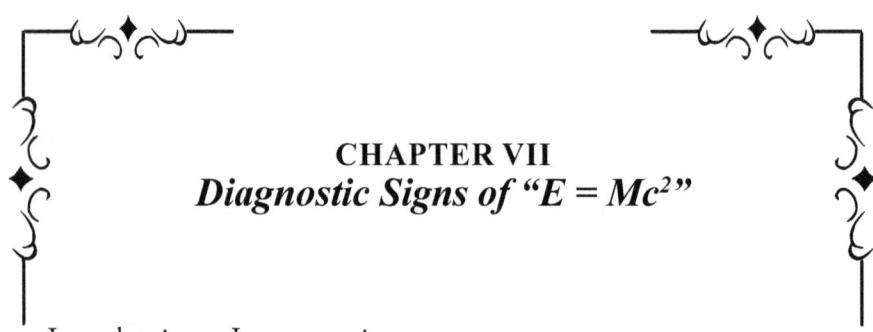

CHAPTER VII
Diagnostic Signs of "E = Mc²"

Introduction – Interpretation:

The following "paper" was submitted to **Nature** May 9, 2006 and received submission approval number 2006-05-04942. Its' cover letter gives the author's e/mail return address as davisfrankeiii@yahoo.com. The actual paper attempts, in a very non-aggressive way, to get the editors of Natureto recognize, by publication, that the equation: $E = Mc^2$ is an inversion of the real perception, since energy (E) and mass (M) have the same mathematical sign in this equation, but are different states of the "transformation" "parity" mass and energy. It carefully avoids openly stating that Einstein and current physicists are exhibiting "ambulatory psychosis" or a split of their perceptual reality by writing the equation with E (energy) as of same sign as M (mass), but could be considered by the sensitive person to do so. The cover letter gives the editors notice of this author's perception, should an "empty response" "without any feedback" occur. Cover Letter: 219 Hunting Ridge Road Roanoke Rapids, North Carolina, 27870 May 9, 2006 Editors of *Nature* www.nature.com/nature/submit/subs

Dear Sirs:

Submitted to you today is the paper "Diagnostic Signs of $E = Mc^2$". This cover letter gives as the reason for submission to Nature that Nature is the most prestigious journal of natural sciences and the author wishes that association. The approximate number of pages in Nature is estimated to be two point two based on 2,857 words or 18,292 characters in the manuscript. I believe the format follows the "Author's Check List".

This copyright-registered paper is submitted, conditionally, to Nature for publication as a physics "insight" article. The condition that at least one reason, related to the equation or theory, be given why the paper is rejected, in the event the paper is rejected, is felt to be reasonable. The reason this request, in the form of a condition, is given, is that my paper " Mathematical Perception of a 'Unified Field Theory' or Its' Loss" in its rejection response was shown no evidence of its' having been read. Such an "empty" response, without any "feedback", allows for no growth in the submission process. The present work, as reduced or "regressed", could be submitted to mathematical, philosophical, physical, or psychoanalytic journals. While it is believed to be best reviewed by professional men, specialized in physics, because of this particular regression of the thought process to such generally recognized and understood phenomena, it can be reviewed in many ways by many specialists. Review by other specialists, of these physical phenomena, would seem to give too much power to those other specialists, regarding the prestige and other perceptions of physicists and *Nature*. Of course, the truthfulness of my work is not dependent upon the perception of any editors and this author is well aware of the bias of Nature against the "unified field theory" of Albert Einstein, as related in Ronald Clark's book on Einstein.[1] Yet, *Nature's* known bias against the theory makes the opinion of *Nature* editors all the more important or helpful, if positive. Please give me some criticism in the event of a rejection, because an "empty" response is perceived as "inadequate to the needs of the situation" and suggests to this author defense of the "fantasy world of brilliance" or the world of "normal science" as suggested by Thomas Kuhn in "Structures of Scientific Revolutions"[2]. This author recognizes himself as a scientific revolutionary and does not covertly present himself as otherwise. Clearly, this author understands the difficulties of this work's presentation and careful review and wishes to be truthful and empathic to *Nature* and its reviewers. While it is not asked for, it is the opinion of this author that *Nature* and its reviewers have real "boundaries" that suggest reviewers should not be paid for opinions of papers without good reasons for those opinions that could be shared with authors, at least in one rational response. In this way, the prestige risk is removed from *Nature* and directed to the responsible opinion maker, who is paid for his opinions.

Yours truly,
Frank E. Davis, III., M.D., FACS davisfrankeiii@yahoo.com
Letter References:

1) Clark, Ronald (1971, 1984), EINSTEIN – The Life and Times (P. 767). Avon Books, An Imprint of Harper and Collins Publishers, 10 East 53rd Street, N.Y., N.Y.

2) Kuhn, Thomas S. (1962, 1970, 1996). **The Structure of Scientific Revolutions**, Third Edition. P.5. University of Chicago Press, Chicago, Illinois, 60637.

Paper submitted: Diagnostic Signs of $E = Mc^2$

"Diagnostic Signs of $E = Mc^2$"

Summary – Introduction:

The "unified field theory" problem has existed at least since Paul Dirac's application of relativity to quantum mechanics in 1925. The problem's solution is variously perceived as the search for a real "hidden variable property" or an unreal "mirage". This paper presents a proposed equation of the problem's solution and the equation's explanation, by theory, that develops a "hidden variable property", EAD, as a real "mirage" (wave-particle image) of an electron's motion characteristics, the real electromagnetic product of mass acceleration-deceleration by energy. This theory is "Particle Electro-Dynamics" (PED) and is called "The Unified Field Theory of 'Charged Particle' Relations and Mass-Energy Transformation(s)". The calculated constant of "equivalent charge of neutral mass" is presented after such a concept of "charge" for "neutral mass" is developed. It is calculated after recognition of "equivalence" of the gravity and Coulomb equations. Subtle suggestion of problems of perception and projection are made, but carefully avoid personal attacks or specific diagnoses. A very global view, not consistent with this paper, could be that, " $E = Mc^2$ should be associated with fission and $Mc^2 = -E$ should be associated with fusion of atoms". The difference is one of perception of energy direction relative to mass and the fact that mass and energy are different entities. Only $Mc^2 = -E$ gives the "unified field".

Manuscript:

If atomic energy can be physically converted to electric energy, and electric energy to electromagnetic and mechanical energies, and mechanical energy to gravity, why does it seem impossible to psychologically and mathematically perceive that all of these energies are part of one energy theory that relates to the mass-energy complex? The reason is because of the "compulsion to associate"[1] ourselves with the equation $E = Mc^2$ when $Mc^2 = -E$. Energy comes from mass by its physical transformation mechanisms. Mass comes from energy by its physical transformation mechanisms. Transformation and normalization equations are unnecessary in the truthful perception of physics, which has true cognizance of the "wave" forms of mass and the "particle" forms of energy. Since mass is a wave of particles and this paper shows that each particle of mass, as atommolecules, generates an EAD "particle" wave image when accelerated or decelerated, classical masses actually generate electro-magnetic wave images of the mass when the mass is accelerated or decelerated. These images, while real, have apparently not been perceived as real. It is important to recognize orbiting masses in "equilibrium" (like planets) as having an equal centripetal acceleration and centripetal deceleration. If mass is transformed to energy, electron-nuclear distance is decreased and "light" or other electromagnetic energy is given off. So that, as electron orbital distance decreases an energy "particle" or "particles" is/are formed and exits the atom-molecule at the velocity of light. If the energy particle is one in number, it is one EAD1. The elemental "particle" of unity for energy, mass, and charge is EADe,m,c respectively. These three unit "particles" are quantitatively one "identity" except that the identity designation is changed depending on whether energy, mass, or charge is the focus of consciousness or direction of propagation. For example, if energy equal to one single EAD (1 EMR of frequency = 1) 6.626×10^{-34} Joules becomes mass by accelerating one electron one "energy level", the mass of that atom-molecule increases by 7.372×10^{-51} kg. ($M = E/c^2$). Notice here how perception of energy-to-mass transformation is conveyed and quantified. The determinate of mass or energy is direction of change of position, in this case relative to the atom-molecule. So, relative to the atom molecule, there is a gain of mass. But, relative to the greater universe there is a loss of energy. A gain of mass is a loss of energy and vice versa. This is an absolute truth, dependent on the position of EADs in mass or in the greater universe. For the "unified field", mass and energy are not thought of as equalities and have opposite sign. EADs in space, or the greater universe, are energy (individual particles) when moving at the v of c, but as a mass of particles form a wave. Because of the limits of the speed of light, their three dimensions (particle v, magnetic, and electrical components), and separate boundaries of EAD "particles", by elastic interference, wavelength is dependent upon frequency. Individual particles of EADs are not augmented by interference waves. The energy of an EAD is "equivalent" to an elemental charge at c (the charge of an electron in quan tity and dependent on direction for +/- quality, with +, relative to a mass, being towards that mass). EADn is a notation for "particle" number and is 1 for "particle" and greater than 1 for a "wave". This paragraph has suggested that if energy types are properly associated and energy understood as to transformation to mass and vice versa, and as an electro-magnetic monopole, with mathematical rigor, a "unified field theory" of massenergy is possible.

The above paragraph shows how sign of E (energy) in the equation, $E = Mc^2$, can invert perception as to mass or energy quality. It also demonstrates that sign is not arbitrary relative to direction as applied to a specific mass. This is a natural "parity". "PED" theory says that: there is a "unified field"; its parities have natural boundaries; and since those parities have real boundaries that are not invertible, perceptual reality is easily inverted in the use of integral transforms. The natural boundary between mass and energy seems to have been lost in Einstein's choice of his "quantum" as a non-unit element "particle". For the equation: $E = hf$, h (Planck's constant) is an "irreducible"[2] and non-integrable "kernel"[3] "element"[4] with boundaries ("irreducible" between integers and with a change of state with change of sign below zero) prohibitive of integration without its subsequent "inversion operation". The integration mechanism, called the "integral transform"[5], requires "inversion"[6] after integration to return the "domain" to reality. The LaPlace transform, used by Heaviside[7], in electromagnetic theory, and the Lorentz transform used in mass-mechanics and gravitational theory require "inversion" "operations" when integrated into Gaussian coordinate systems as domains, to maintain a true, non-inverted awareness of state of the X,Y elements of the integrations. For electromagnetism, the inversion is from wave to mass of charge. For the Lorentz transform the inversion is from energy to mass of objects. So, the apparently duplicitous position that "mass changes the space about it"[8] exhibiting perception of space as a "cloth"[9,10]-like material, while denying the material existence of an ether, is explained by gravity's true relationship to the equilibrium, mass to energy and energy to mass, described by the gravitational constant and perceived as mass giving energy (electric or magnetic) when acted upon by physical forces (electric or magnetic). In the case of gravity, masses give up EADc "charged particles" in response to other masses giving up similar "charged particles" moving in the opposite direction or towards them. Thus, as one atom-molecule system (mass-wave) de-saturates its receptors to the other, the second (mass or wave) or "greater universe" de-saturates to the first. Gravity is not caused by mass changing the space about it, but is a dissociation of mass to energy. So that the gravity force is energy/distance or F = E/d. Einstein was apparently expressing an inversion of perception of mass for energy. This perceptual inversion is another cause of loss of the "unified field". Atom-molecules are "intrinsic semiconductors" that respond to "stimulant" energy forms with electron acceleration, recognized in this paper as increased mass, and to the greater universe negative energy projection (or + physical forces and entropy) with EAD loss or energy transfer (from mass to energy by "natural transforms"). Electro-magnetic fields of "charged particles" (really EADs or EMR) result from physical force or EAD energy over distance applied to atom-molecules, and also result when those molecules have velocity changes (inertia) and when those molecules have constant centripetal acceleration-deceleration complements (gravity). "PED" grants the requisite mono-polar electro-magnetic charge(s), EADs, having charge dependent upon direction of motion relative to the mass in question and negative towards the "greater universe".

It is a paradox that the constant c must be associated with M (mass) to obtain E (energy) in the equation: $Mc^2 = -E$, because it is E that has the v (velocity) of c (speed of light). That the E and M segments of this equation should have opposite signs should be obvious to all reasonable persons. The "compulsion to associate" like charges with E (energy) and Mass (mass) is indicative of a "false alliance"[11] probably by "transference" caused by mathematicians not understanding physics or physicians not understanding mathematics. But, it could be a result of physicists'(s) not understanding physical phenomena due to "inversion"(s). That is suggested by Einstein's "cloth" perception of gravity as mass deforming space and by the positive energy sign. Reality perception of the "unified field" results from "identification" of the EADn,e,m,c"particle", its' four elementary dimensions, and their developments. It is only with that perception and its' "logic of relations"[12] that the "unified field" is seen as a physical reality and its equation projected. Since reality is found, and not defined, if these equation segments express the change of mass properly with the proper gain of energy of separation, they are likely to be immutable, except by equivalent changes of segments or more extensive application(s). Whatever the proper equation to express it, unity of the physical functions of the universe and its perception is cognizance of the EAD element or its symbolic equivalents. This reality is unlikely to change. "The Equation" of Particle Electro-Dynamics (PED) is: (For the atom(s)): $\Delta Mc^2 = \Delta E =$ (For the "Particle (n = 1)" or "waves $(n)1)$") $= EADn$ x -EADe = EADn x EADm x c^2 = (The unity derivative) +/- EADn x EADc at velocity c = (For Gravity): $1/2(G((M1M2/d1^2) + (M1\Delta M2\Delta/d2^2)))$ x Δd (all Δs require some mathematical and personal tolerance) = (For Electromagnetism): $1/2(K((q1q2/d1^2) + (q1\Delta q2\Delta/d2^2)))$ x Δd

Discussion of the equation:

First the negative sign, for all particles of energy, is the sign required for designation of energy as opposed to mass. This concept can be very confusing as Bohr said, "If anybody says he can think about quantum problems without getting gitty, that only shows he has not understood the first thing about them".[13] The parity, or mirror complement of that is Pauling, who said, "There is no danger of confusion".[14] Notice the EADm does not have the negative sign and demonstrates change from the energy to the mass state by transformation from energy of the "greater universe" to "equivalent mass" of the "greater atom-molecule" by increased bi-polarity of that atom-molecule. This mechanism is consistent with the author's previously stated position that, "Gravity results from mutual atomic-molecular polarity". The perception of this author is that the EAD is Dirac's magnetic "monopole". This magnetic monopole is positive when directionally moving towards a given mass in question and negative when moving away from that conscious reference center of mass. EADs are either positive towards a given mass or negative away from it. The negative sign for energy is required to demonstrate, in the mathematical projection, that mass of this projection of reality comes from loss of energy and energy comes from the loss of mass. This is another way of saying, "There is no free lunch." The EADn,e,m,c are for, respectively: number, energy, "equivalent mass", and "equivalent charge" at c. The mass and charge equivalents are ninety-degree electromagnetic parities (magnetic or electric, respectively). For the M (mass) and q (charge) quantities of the gravitation and electromagnetic segments there are almost undetectable changes of mass and/or charge in changed position states (Δd or change in distance). But, the changes, consistent with "PED", are inversions of Heaviside and Einstein who, both, used integral transforms (Heaviside, first, with the LaPlace transform and Einstein, with the Lorentz transformation). For this publication E, M, G, and K are generally accepted notations for energy, mass, gravitational constant, and Coulomb's constant. The EAD is found in nature as the elementary unit of "mass", energy, and unit "charge". The letters stand for "extra analytic detail" or "Elizabeth Anne Davis". EADs are detectable in nature as EMR by the physical technique of spectroscopy. The equation segments must be interpreted as domains of "rings of integers" and do not deny other real phenomena, but do suggest, by description, nonlinear functions or functions with holes between integers, due to the real quantum nature of energy phenomena. Δs (deltas) or changes might be required for this equation to project this theory. This author is certainly no mathematician. The issue of these charge and mass quantity changes does raise several parity issues. The focus of consciousness should now be kinetic versus potential energy. "PED" perceives potential energy as mass and kinetic energy as energy and recognizes complementarity, but also "hidden variables". Classical and relative physics is not conscious of EADS and mass-energy transformation at the unit level, therefore this equation could represent a "split" in my state of conscious between relative and classical physics and "PED". It could be possible that the important force is not the average force, as written, but the proper force could be the change in force. At this time, the author requests your patience and assistance. Please help me express this true theory "with truthful mathematical rigor"!

Once the EAD as an electro-magnetically induced, directionally specific, electro-magnetic monopole, associated with "valence bands"[15] of atom-molecules as "intrinsic semiconductors"[16] or the greater universe is understood, the Maxwell equations[17] link or string together gravity and electro-magnetism. An "equivalent charge for neutral mass" (Dc) is then calculated as 8.61646 x 10-[11] Coulombs/kg. using F (force) of gravity equal to F of Coulomb's force for "neutral mass equivalence". "PED" "Mirrors" or "Parities" of "Symmetry": "PED" is best understood by recognizing "limits" as natural phenomena with complements, mirror images, parities, and/or the universe as having "symmetry". The "kernel" limit is c, the speed of light. This is a unity parity because its' derivative is one. Time and distance are both determined by c. It causes gravity or "mutual atomic-molecular polarity" by its upper and lower limits as well as the limit of r (that Dr. Witten is circling). The constancy of c forces "mutual atomic-molecular polarities" for universal bodies in motion because the electron clouds shift to the rear of moving molecules giving bi-polarity and effective bipolar masses (waves) of bipolar atom-molecules. Masses are like magnets in motion due to c as an upper and lower limit (e-m waves travel at c regardless of the electron's v). Now the mirror of c is h, expressed solely as energy or the EAD energy of the e-m mirror-image parity of the electron's motion at whatever v! An elemental charge is not only an electron, but it is also its' wave complement, the EAD. The e-m wave complements of the electron have ninetydegree parities, so the EAD is properly viewed as energy or charge, and by natural transformation as mass. It all fits like a glove. If it fits, you must be bits. You are a part of light! This theory or explanation of the way the universe functions was developed by recognizing that Albert Einstein devalued himself and his own finding of the constancy of c, the speed of light. Sometimes we do not recognize our own greatness.

"PED" Findings:

1. Application of Maxwell's theory, as understood by "PED", explains the "photoelectric effect" as a displacement of an electron charge by the "parity energy wave-particle" of a prior or complementary electron's deceleration. It is called a wave because it is formed by motion of a charged particle (electron) but has unit EAD1 quality because of unit charge deceleration as its' cause. High frequency represents shortened time of acceleration-deceleration for electrons and time between EADS, but each EAD works the same way. This is why photons of high frequency have high energies. There are just more EADS! The frequency has to be high to have the narrow h distance or λchange, another paradox, but

the phenomenon is the same for all electron acceleration-decelerations by EADs (EADe to m, EADm to e).

2. Acceleration-deceleration of all masses produces EADs. Pressure forces EADs out as does temperature, but low ambient temperature pulls EADs out and promotes fusion or Einstein's "congealment", another "symmetry" or complementary limit.

3. Because loss of EADs gives greater density and is associated with greater entropy: a) Black holes may be "big bangs" in preparation and b) Fusion reactions, paradoxically, but by complementarity, may be assisted by super-cooling! It appears that "critical mass" by fission is the complementary parity of "critical mass" by fusion.

4. The "r" of the atom cannot vanish because the force of positive (+) charge for an electron's centripetal deceleration equals its negative electrical charge (magnetic and electric are parities). The wave is "equal and opposite" the charge by electro-magnetic complementarity, symmetry, or parity. This relates Maxwell's fourth equation and is a "balance of *Nature*" where $r = dD/dt$ (r is c dependent due to v of c for e-m radiations or EADc,e velocities) and J = current density of 0 or equality, so that curl of H is "constant", due to balance of electric and magnetic forces.

References for Chapter VII:

1 Freud, Sigmund (1895). "Psychotherapy of Hysteria". S.E. 2: Pp. 301-305.

2 "Irreducible" element. Source, The New Encyclopedia Britannica, 15[thth] 295. McHenry, Robert, General Editor; Chicago.

3 " Kernel". Ibid 2, V 6: P337.

4 "Unity", "Ring of Integers". Source: Ibid 2, P. 294.

5 Ibid. 3.

6 Op. Cite.

7 Ibid 2: V. 5, P. 789.

8 "Mass changes space about it." Source: Zitzewitz, Paul W. Neff, Robert F. Davids, Mark (1995). Merrill **Physics** Principles and Problems P. 169. Glencoe/McGraw-Hill N.Y., N.Y.

9 "Cloth". *Nature*, October 9, 1975 quote from de Sitter letter.

10 Clark, Ronald (1971, 1984), EINSTEIN – The Life and Times (P. 772). Avon Books, An Imprint of Harper and Collins Publishers, 10 East 53rd Street, N.Y., N.Y.

11 Ibid. 1.

12 Piaget, Jean (1937), "Principle Factors Determining Intellectual Evolution From Childhood to Adult Life", from Rapaport, David (1951, 1956, 1959), ORGANIZATION AND PATHOLOGY OF THOUGHT: Selected Sources, Pp. 154-192. Columbia University Press, N.Y.

13 Bohr's "Gitty". Ibid. 8 P. 558.

14 Pauling's "no danger of confusion". Pauling, Linus (1935, 1963). Introduction to **Quantum Mechanics** With Applications to Chemistry (428-436). General Publishing Company, Ltd. 30 Lesmill Road, Don Mills, Toronto, Ontario, Canada.

15 "Valence Bands". Ibid 8, P. 598.

16 "Intrinsic semiconductors". Ibid. 8, P. 600.

17 Maxwell Equations, Ibid 2 V. 7, Pp. 968-969.

CHAPTER VIII
Particle Electro-Dynamics (PED): Confirmation of Einstein's Unified Field With Mathematical Rigor

Introduction – Interpretation:

This "paper" was submitted to the journal *Nature* May 24, 2006 at 10:47 A.M. and received the manuscript number 2006-05-05606. It specifically uses the term "inversions" of perception, in its' abstract, and suggests the true "kernel element" of physical perception (the EAD) leads to perception of the "unified field" and conscious "identification" of the "strings" of "String Theory". The cover letter to the "Editors of *Nature*" informs those editors that it is this author's intention to publish a book that suggests delay in finding the "unified field" and its equation results from "ego-centrism" with the ego determined to be a "feeling of knowing" (or fantasy world of brilliance). Again, as for the "paper" "Diagnostic Signs of $E = Mc^2$, this cover letter requests a focused "feedback", "even if the paper is rejected". There is, of course, application of Maxwell's equations in the presentation of this paper. At the time of presentation of this paper, no response to the "Diagnostic Signs of $E = Mc^2$ paper had been received. This was two weeks after that paper's presentation. Again this cover letter gives the e/mail address of its author as davisfrankeiii@yahoo.com. The author must relate, to the readers of this book *the very strong negative feelings that he has towards the editor(s) of Nature for not addressing the theses of his papers, despite his specific and pointed requests that they do so*. To the author's perception, and probably for readers of this book, these editors "hold themselves out" as "knowing" persons of science and, at the same time, refuse to be "stand up guys" in a case of monumental importance to science. Of course, they appear to be "charming and engaging" in the process. The author's admitted feelings could be used to "identify" him as a "negative" or "hateful" person, but they are explained, in this case to result from "the negative transference" of those editors and would be predicted by proper application of Freud's work to this situation and would lead to a proper "identification" of the editors, themselves. Of course, for this author, his understanding that the opinions of the editors of Nature do not effect his reality perception, without careful scrutiny, modifies those "negative feelings". But you see, reader(s), their value system does effect what you read in their journal! Finally, on June 20, 2006, but only after sending a request inquiring as to why the papers, "Diagnostic Signs of $E = Mc^2$" and "Particle Electro-Dynamics...", had not been recognized as received, did I receive the following response to these papers:

"Dear Dr. Davis,

Thank you for your email. In our database we have this email address for you, davisfranke@yahoo.com, this will be the reason why you did not receive the receipts and decision letters of your two manuscripts. I have now added this email address davisfrankeiii@yahoo.com to our records as well as keeping the old one. A decision has been made on both your manuscripts and below is the original decision letter:

Dear Dr Davis

Thank you for submitting your manuscript, which we are regretfully unable to publish.

It is Nature's policy to return a substantial proportion of manuscripts without sending them to referees, so that they may be sent elsewhere without delay. Decisions of this kind are made by the editorial staff when it appears that papers are unlikely to succeed in the competition for limited space.

In the present case, while your findings may well prove stimulating to others' thinking about such questions, I regret that we are unable to conclude that the work provides the sort of firm advance in general understanding that would warrant publication in Nature. We therefore feel that the paper would find a more suitable outlet in a specialist journal. I am sorry that we cannot respond more positively on this occasion, but I hope that you will rapidly receive a more favorable response elsewhere. Yours sincerely

Nature Administration

We send our apologies and hope the delay did not cause you any inconvenience.

Kind Regards"

Interpretation (continued):

This was certainly a "charming" response that "failed to meet the needs of the situation" as to the truthfulness of whether these short papers explain Einstein's loss of the "unified field", mathematically.

Cover Letter:

219 Hunting Ridge Road

Roanoke Rapids, North Carolina, 27870 May 24, 2006

Editors of Nature www.nature.com/nature/submit/subs

Dear Sirs:

Submitted to you is the paper "Particle Electro-Dynamics (PED): Confirmation of Einstein's Unified Field With Mathematical Rigor". The reason for submission of this paper to Nature is that it is this author's opinion that *Nature* is the most prestigious journal of the natural sciences and that association is desired for this paper and this author's work. The approximate number of pages in *Nature* is estimated to be 3.66 based on 4,756 words or 26,463 characters (without space count) in the manuscript, excluding references. While reference number is 32, reference sources number only ten, as most are used more than once. Aside from the number of references and possibly the number of words, it is believed this paper meets the author's checklist requirements. Clearly, if this paper meets its objective, it should be strongly considered for publication and its denial would be a loss for the journal *Nature*, as well as others. The editorial strength, as well as prestige, of *Nature* is vigorously sought and truthfully courted.

This author has considerable confidence that he has now, mathematically, solved the problems of presentation for the "unified field" and that he is able to defend its herein presented perception. For that reason and the known importance of such a proof, the author is today filing for registration of copyright of this work with the U.S. Copyright Office. Clearly, if the editors of *Nature* agree with the real value of this work, this author will transfer copyright to the journal for such "peer-reviewed publication". This author does believe he has real, document able, financial interests in publication of his work in *Nature*, or its denial of publication, but recognizes only benefits if it is denied publication for real reasons of physics. Because the author always attempts to be truthful, he sees no conflict of interest in the fact that he is writing a book that suggests that delay in solving the "unified field" problem resulted(s) from the same "ego-centrism" that has delayed all other scientific advancements, a feeling of "knowing". Because of the great effort expended in presentation of this work and the value of its motivational truth, if real, this author feels it reasonable, for both the editors and this author, that the editors of *Nature* give some "feedback", even if the paper is rejected.

This paper, while similar to the "Diagnostic Signs of E = Mc²" paper, sharpens the mathematical argument with discovered partition constants and application of Maxwell's equations and pointedly reveals the diagnosis, previously not mentioned. It was actually written prior to the "Diagnostic Signs of E = Mc²" paper, but was previously felt to be too insensitive for presentation.

Yours truly,

Frank E. Davis, III., M.D., FACS davisfrankeiii@yahoo.com

Paper: *Particle Electro-Dynamics (PED): Confirmation of Einstein's Unified Field with Mathematical Rigor* "Particle Electro-Dynamics" (PED) Confirmation of Einstein's "Unified Field" With "Mathematical Rigor"

Summary-Introduction-Caution: This paper concerns very controversial, but important, issues of physics for which a final solution is not generally accepted. Finding one error in such an important pursuit or work does not justify its abandonment and at least one error is almost inevitable. Inversions of perception are assumed to be real for everyone, occasionally, and are to be dealt with patiently and with respect. It is hoped that the attitude of patience and respect is perceived in this work and its' reading and review. There should be no doubt that reasonable and informed people can resolve any perceptual inversions with physical reality and find its' mathematical description to equal that truthful perception. This paper seeks that difficult, but rewarding, accomplishment.

The search for the "unified field" has been long and difficult, with many intelligent and well-informed persons sharing the belief that unity is, or would be, mathematically impossible. Yet, by finding the "unity element" or mathematical "kernel element" hidden in plain sight by the ego-centric fantasy perception of "knowing", this paper submits a "unified field" equation and unifies gravity and electromagnetism with application of Maxwell's equations to gravity as perceived with "Particle Electro-Dynamics". In effect successful application of

Maxwell's equations to the "PED" theory of gravity is proof of that theory, because it is the only available theory that explains both gravity and inertia as quantitatively measurable forces, rather than deformation of a non-"ether" "cloth"-like space by mass "strings". If you wish, this paper "identifies" those "strings".

Manuscript:

While successful application of Quantum Electro-Dynamics (QED) and Relativity theories resulting mainly from Einstein, as suggested by findings of Newton, Maxwell, Planck, Lorentz, and particularly with Minkowski, associated with further mathematical developments by P.A.M. Dirac and R. Feynman is undeniable, the current situation denies the core belief of Einstein that there exists a "unified field" that can be expressed with a single equation or "one formula"[1]. Development of understanding of the physical world that will allow truthful expression with such an equation is said to be the core goal of physics today. That understanding seems to require an element common to the three theories of physics that has been variously described as "a hidden variable"[2] or "unknown property"[3] whose real existence is perceived as like a "mirage"[4]. Albert Einstein looked diligently for this "identity" from about 1916 until his death in 1955. No person in world history has done more to establish the value of "identity equations" than Albert Einstein and thus the value of mathematics as a tool of the consummate scientist. While it may not be a generally accepted view, it appears that the scientist most-respected and loved of all time is, Albert Einstein. The reason(s) supportive of that view is (are) that: 1) Albert Einstein's thought dominates physics in both General Relativity and Quantum ElectroDynamics and seems to be a perceptual reality that has been defended, despite risks to its defenders; 2) Because mathematics is dependent upon its usefulness to others for its reality, mathematics, itself, has been perceptually effected by Einstein's perceptions; 3) While Einstein specifically denied the relevance of "Relativity" to thought in "domains" other than physics, relative perception, rather than absolute perception, has become the norm of "world views" now. Despite this perception of Einstein's great prestige, his personal perceptual dominance, and this author's affection for Einstein's public image and person, it is apparent that we lost the "unified field" when Albert Einstein "particle"-"quantized" Planck's work as "$E = hf$", without finding the energy value and other "equivalent properties" for an energy frequency of one ("particle"), leading to linear mathematical perception of a discontinuous, incremental, and intermittent physical "step" process best thought of mathematically as a "step function" for a "ring of integers"[5]with h, Planck's constant, as its' unity factor (u). But, this alone was probably not enough to cause the present situation. His thought is so dominant in physics that not only does he have many people mathematically perceiving mass-energy transformations as continuous and uninterrupted functions, but he also has many people believing gravity is a "change of (an "ether"[6]-like "sheet"[7] or "cloth"-like[8]) space by mass"[9] (Parentheses mine). Further, I have heard lay people say, "Einstein proved mass is energy" or that, "Mass and energy are equivalent". One college physics book[10] states that $\Delta E = (\Delta M)c^2$ is "so well proven" that the "law of conservation of energy" "by extrapolation and as a matter of scientific faith" should be "assumed to apply to the entire universe" and exhibits its lack of recognition of the "partition boundary" of mass and energy with the term "massergy". Such a "logic of relations"[11] and lack of truthful "identification", in a college textbook, should be viewed as disgraceful, if its' author simultaneously denies "faith" in entities other than "science". This paper demonstrates that recognizing the natural difference of mass and energy, "wave" and "particle", leads to reality perception of the unified field.

There is a category of medical disorders that is characterized with a "compulsion to associate" even opposite qualities as related or "relative" to each other. A person exhibiting such a disorder appears very eccentric, but may be "very charming and engaging". Since human perception and habits of dealing with physical phenomena is a learned coordination of self with the world, projected associations are often verbally learned perceptions, especially in science. In the science of physics the projected associations are by equations. This paper submits that the most obvious reason that we currently do not have an understanding of the "unified field" perception and equation is because Albert Einstein perceived "$E = Mc^2$" instead of "$Mc^2 = -E$". Now, a charming and engaging personality will not "make waves" about such a "detail", but this author believes all readers of this paper know that M (mass) results from E (energy) loss or vice versa. This means M (mass) and E (energy) are complements or parities of nature and mathematical "associates"[12], but have opposite direction or charge and, therefore, sign in this equation. The true "identity" or "identification" is that consumption of mass yields energy. Since "rings of integers"[13] require "association"[14] of different "elements"[15] for a "domain" to be defined, perceptual reality can be inverted by the direction traveled (or by application of the wrong sign to the physically real direction) in a "ring of integral multiples"[16] or "elements" of a real unitary value perceived or not perceived as a "unit element"[18]. This inversion of perception of reality can then be "transformed"[19] or caused, mathematically, with equations of "transformation" or "renormalization" that "defend"[20] one from the reality of one's perceptual inversion, or prevent reality perception and cause other perceptual problems in "symmetry"[21]. The words used in mathematics do not necessarily have the same meaning that they have in common parlance, but should have if there is unity of mathematical projection, perception, and reality. So that, "cyclic reasoning" or "rings" map "domains" of pure math and do not indicate improper thought, but mandate the "domain of thought" must "map with" the "domain of reality" and not its mirror image or "inversion". This is the domain's directional (vector) quality that gives spatial or state (mass versus energy) orientation. It should be recognized by all persons, knowledgeable in physics, that directional parity in electromagnetism is in ninety-degree relationships, rather than the usual 180-degree habitual perception. A person who developed such equations of inverted perception could have been ignorant of physical phenomena by perceptual deficit or by learning inverted perceptual "associations" as mathematically defined[22] ($E = Mc^2$) rather than as discoverable in nature ($Mc^2 = -E$). Since physics has become perception by mathematics, and involves "transformation" and "renormalization equations", incorrectly learned perceptual associations may have been mathematically induced. Albert Einstein's mathematics professor at the ETH, Dr. Minkowski, was not impressed with Albert Einstein's mathematical ability or work[23]. Even Albert Einstein said, "I am no Einstein". Of course, he meant by that statement that the public "over-idealized" his brilliance. This paper cites these negative comments from others as true revelations of theirperception of the professor's image, but attempts to make only positive statements about Einstein. Yet, the wording could be more humorous and possibly more "charming and engaging", if negative. But, the "gravity" of the situation requires a humble submission to love of others and the truth that: $Mc^2 = -E$.

Particle Electro-Dynamics (PED) is different from Quantum Electro-Dynamics (QED) as to "uncertainty" or "indeterminacy" and upholds Professor Einstein's greater view of the universe as a "unified field". PED does not require "transformation equations" or "renormalization equations", but does view nature as having normalcy in transformation of energy to mass (matter) and mass (matter) to energy, rather than expressing their "relativity" or "equivalence". "The Equation" of Particle Electro-Dynamics is: (For the atom(s)): $\Delta Mc^2 = \Delta E =$ (For the "Particle (n = 1)" or "waves (n)1)"") = EADn x -EADe = EADn x EADm x c^2 = EADn x -/+EADc at velocity c (dependent on direction towards a specific mass) = (For Gravity): $1/2(G((M1M2/d1^2) + (M1\Delta M2\Delta/d2^2)))$ x Δd = (For Electromagnetism): $1/2(K((q1q2/d1^2) + (q1\Delta q2\Delta/d2^2)))$ x Δd Discussion of the equation:

First the negative sign, for all particles of energy, is the sign required for designation of energy as opposed to mass. This concept can be very confusing as Bohr said, "If anybody says he can think about quantum problems without getting gitty, that only shows he has not understood the first thing about them"[24]. The parity, or mirror complement of that is Pauling, who said, "There is no danger of confusion"[25]. The EAD "particle" is the parity unit wave complement of a valence electron's motion as acceleration or deceleration. Said differently, it is the wave complement of an electron's charged particle motion, position, change in position, or change in rate of change of position (acceleration or deceleration). Its' energy is found, mathematically, in one of two ways (both of which require recognition of unity of perception with reality): 1) Graphically by reading Planck's data graph at the frequency of one (unit frequency). 2) Solving the algebraic equation for energy for frequency of one when the energy is known for any other frequency. The EAD1, where n = 1 is one EMR and has energy = 6.626×10^{-34} Joules and in that perception is EAD1e. The EADm is the mass equivalent of EAD1e energy and equals $-EAD1e/c^2$ or 7.372×10^{-51} kg. The EADc is a unit charge at c (the speed of light) and is positive when moving towards a given mass and negative when moving away from a given mass. EADn is the number of EADs and is one (unity) unless otherwise specified. Notice the EADm does not have the negative sign and demonstrates change from the energy to the mass state by transformation from energy of the "greater universe"[26] to "equivalent mass" of the "greater atom-molecule" by increased bi-polarity of that atom-molecule. This mechanism is consistent with the author's previously stated position that, "Gravity results from mutual atomicmolecular polarity". The perception of this author is that the EAD is Dirac's magnetic "monopole". This magnetic monopole is positive when directionally moving towards a given mass in question and negative when moving away from that conscious reference center of mass. EADs are either positive towards a given mass or negative away from it. The negative sign for energy is required to demonstrate, in the mathematical projection, that mass of this projection of reality comes from loss of energy and energy comes from the loss of mass. This is another way of saying, "There is no free lunch." The $EAD_{n,e,m,c}$ are for, respectively: number, energy, "equivalent mass", and "equivalent charge" at c (the speed of light). The mass and charge equivalents are ninety-degree electromagnetic parities (magnetic or electric, respectively). For the M (mass) and q (charge) quantities of the gravitation and electromagnetic segments there are almost undetectable changes of mass and/or charge in changed position states (Δd or change in distance). But, the changes, consistent with "PED", are inversions of Heaviside and Einstein who, both, used integral transforms (Heaviside, first, with the LaPlace transform and Einstein, with the Lorentz transformation). For this publication E, M, G, and K are generally accepted notations for energy, mass, gravitational constant, and Coulomb's constant, respectively. The EAD is found in nature as the elementary unit of "mass", energy, and unit "charge". The letters stand for "extra analytic detail" or "Elizabeth Anne Davis". EADs are detectable in nature as EMR (electro-magnetic radiation(s)) by the physical technique of spectroscopy. The equation segments must be interpreted as "domains" of "rings of integers" and do not deny other real phenomena, but are mandated by Planck's data to be nonlinear "step functions" or functions with "excluded middles" between integers, due to the real quantum nature of energy phenomena. Particular difficulties arise in attempts to use integral calculus with Gaussian "domains" due to direction losses when squaring and finding square routes of qualities of different sign that are of one continuum. Because of the apparent novelty of this perception, the author must specifically mention the opposite signs required for energy and mass as part of one 90-degree parity often thought of as a 180-degree parity. Δs (deltas) or changes might be required for this equation to project this theory. This author is certainly no mathematician. The issue of the charge and mass quantity changes of these equation segments does raise several parity issues. The focus of consciousness should now be kinetic versus potential energy. "PED" perceives potential energy as mass and kinetic energy as energy and recognizes complementarity, but also "hidden variables". Classical and relative physics is not conscious of EADS and mass-energy transformation at the unit level, therefore this equation could represent a "split" in state of consciousness between relative and classical physics and "PED". It could be possible that the important force is not the average force, as written, but the proper force could be the change in force. At this time, the author requests your patience and assistance. The appeal of this paper is, "Help express this true theory with truthful mathematical rigor"!

The "PED" Explanation (Theory) of Gravity:

Atom-molecules are "capacitors" or "intrinsic semiconductors" capable of holding energy as "effective positive charge(s)" in their "valence layers". This energy is also "effective mass". Energy in the valence layer of atommolecules should be regarded as mass after energy-to-mass transformation. The absence of energy in a "hole" of the valence layer is an entropy capacitor or capacity of that atom-molecule for energy (nominally, an AMD). Either energy's presence in the valence layer or an accelerated electron (at higher "energy level") is evidence of received energy (EADS or EMR) from other sources and is a "stimulant" for EAD release for that atom-molecule by "decay" towards the nucleus of accelerated electrons of atom-molecules. Receipt of an incoming EAD "particle" of energy as a valence layer "particle" of "mass" (or mirror-parity "charge" through ninety-degree parity understanding of electromagnetism) causes electron "energy level" shift (or acceleration understood as going to a "higher energy level") or, of course, electron loss from the atom-molecule. But, yet another phenomenon, recognized by Einstein, is that sometimes energy that enters an atom-molecule in sequential couplets leads to loss of energy equal to both quanta of the couplet. This is termed "stimulated emission". "Stimulated emission", of energy rather than an electron, is explained in "PED" as deceleration of the electron by reverse opening of the "hole" (AMD receptor potential) for escape of positive energy (due to spin) with subsequent release of energy, rather than the negative electron and suggests parity in valence band receptors (AMDs) as well as parity of electrons in conduction bands that open AMD receptor sights. Receipt or loss of valence layer or valence band energy-"mass" results in a 90-degree shift of the valence layer "hole" (by laws of electromagnetism). Passage of an electron into a "lower energy level" closes the "hole" of electron passage and opens a valence receptor (AMD), while entrance of an EAD into the valence layer (AMD) opens the hole for electron passage, again with 90-degree parity. Thus entrance of "mass"(often thought of as energy) to the valence layer lengthens the magnetic dipole of the atom-molecule and its loss (as energy) shortens the magnetic dipole. Electron deceleration or drop in "energy level" produces energy "particles" that "diverge" to other atom-molecules as EADs following geodesic curves. The magnetic state of an atom-molecule (gravity) appears to be one of valence shell energy absence or entropy capacity so that electrons of that mass are insulated from the greater universe (by AMD receptors). But the electromotive state of atom-molecules (inertia) exposes electrons to the "greater universe" by a "hole" in the valence layer caused by the presence of an energy particle, locally (AMD receptor filling with energy). Since the holes in the valence layer or band are caused by receipt of energy received perpendicular to the direction of motion, the "charge(s)" or images of that energy move in the direction of motion and is (are) identified with inertia. This concept of the "outer valence layer" as a "structure" functioning for the atom-molecule as a "signal receptor" or transducer is surprisingly similar to "signal transduction receptors" and "signal transduction pathways" of the "cell membrane(s)" of living cells, but was developed entirely from separate linkages of thought that have just been described here. In a separate copyrighted paper, this author has suggested that sensory receptors of living organisms, cells, function as structures that associate "stimulation" to time and/or frequency and labeled the receptor sites that function by frequency association with time as AMD [27]s. This is in agreement with the Brouwer intuitionist mathematical theory that human perception is linked to time perception, but not in agreement with its projection that mathematics requires "continuous middles" and denies "step functions", because mathematics can be shown to be more complete in inclusion and exclusion than human perception(s). Entropy and deceleration state numbers are directly related to atom-molecule mass and appear to be two per orbital for all orbitals. "Effective charge" of "neutral mass" is calculated to be 8.61646 x 10^{-11} Coulombs/kg (Dc). There is mutual equilibrium of loss of EAD energy and its gain by any two masses in gravitational relationship(s). Gravitational and Coulomb constants are effectively dissociation constants of mass to energy and charge to energy, respectively, with v (velocity) of c (speed of light). These constants are essentially inversions of mass-charge densities over space and are "dissociation" constants (rather than compulsive associations) suggesting the EAD is not a variable defined physical "constant", like the "photon" but is a "hidden variable" or "unknown property", hidden in plain sight. Its' "variability" relates to the frequency of mass-to-energy or energy-to-mass transformations, during various physical events or "happenings", and its' state, determined by velocity (charge and mass or energy). Critical energy becomes mass when its' velocity needs to exceed c, the speed of light, but cannot." "The Unified Field" perception requires recognition of 6.626 x 10^{-34} Joules as a fundamental or elemental property of one electromagnetic radiation or EAD1. This fundamental property, EADe, or elementary "particle" EAD1, has a "mirage"-like elemental charge or the unit of charge of quantity equal to + 1.6022 x 10^{-19} Coulomb(s) (EADc, found mathematically by calculating charge at c required to yield 6.626 x 10$^{-34 \text{ Joules energy}}$ and searched for because energy is not supposed to have mass), and a mathematically "equivalent mass" of 7.372 x 10^{-51} kg. (EADmfound mathematically by $M = -E/c^2$(at velocity c, with direction positive (+) towards unity of mass or charge). Gravity is not a result of "mass changing the space about it"[28] because the conceptualization exhibits perception of space as a "cloth"[29,30]-like "ether" space, but is a force caused by the mutual exchange of EADs (energy particles over space-distance) that result from losses of electron "energy levels", giving wave images, EADs, that enter atom-molecules at the v of c as electromagnetic radiation(s) or particle(s) of waves. This links the author, perceptually, to Feynman diagrams as wave-particle perceptions. Clearly, perception of energy as a "particle" is difficult for most people, even when trained to do so. For all "photon" "particles" of my experience, what is being talked about is a "wave". This leads to "particle"-"wave" inversion and often mass-energy inversion. While not generally appreciated, there is a natural "partition boundary" of the "particle". This paper develops the EAD "particle" in dimensions of energy, "equivalent charge", "equivalent mass", and number(s) as a "particle" (1) or "wave" ()1).

"PED" theory suggests the explanation for inertia is related to perception of atom-molecules as "intrinsic semiconductors" whose "valence band" "holes", or AMDs, are emptied by negative acceleration, or acceleration away from the mass or charge in question, and filled by positive acceleration (towards mass or charge as mass). Thus, inertia is resistance to change in state of motion (presence or absence) by electromotive force(s) of quantity $F = E/d$, with E resulting from dissociation of mass by physical force of an "equal and opposite" nature. Physical (magnetic) and electrical (electromotive) forces have mirror parity from complementary masses that can be confusing to this author. Physical (gravitational, magnetic) forces pull or push EADs out, while electromotive forces drive EADs toward complementary masses. This explains the inversional perception(s) of Heaviside and Einstein regarding " increases" of charge-mass as v (velocity) approaches c (speed of light) as due to inversion of charge and mass versus energy perception. Rapid deceleration at impact from falls clearly causes fission of mass(es) into fragments with significant fragmentation energy consumption.

"PED" theory suggests gravity and inertia can be described with Maxwell's equations of electromagnetism. Gravity is perceived as the force of magnetism. Inertia is perceived as the electromotive force or its complementary "equal and opposite". Notice the ninety-degree parity(s) of gravity and inertia with each other. These parities are ninety degrees to each other and to direction of motion of the masses of gravitational phenomena. The reader will say, "Not exactly". This is because of "geodesic" curves of the electromagnetic wave(s) and the force "field" concept. Inertia is seen in the Maxwell equations31as an electric force with "divergence" equal to charge density resulting from centrifugal acceleration that causes a loss of EADs from the accelerated mass and gain of EADs to the other mass or greater universe. The cause of the EAD loss(es) is the cause of the centrifugal acceleration (previously an unconscious force).

1) Mathematically: Div of D = p. The gravitational field is uniform between the two objects and does not diverge because of its' cause by uniform geodesic motion of "charged neutral masses" (Dc= 8.61646 x 10-11 Coulombs/kg.). 2) Mathematically: Div B = 0.

The electromotive force of inertia opposes acceleration or deceleration of both masses because of a requirement for change in the EAD states from saturated to open AMD sites, or unsaturated to closed AMD sites, respectively. Inertia is both the negative mass-producing force for acceleration and the negative energyproducing force for deceleration. Its curl gives direct opposition of motion changes by geodesic curvature of force field. 3) Mathematically: Curl E = -dB/dt.

The magnetic or gravitational field has curl resulting from the electric field (of EADs) and/or flow of EADs from one mass to the other by geodesic curves due to charged particle motions. 4) Mathematically: Curl H = dD/dt + J. This is the most interesting finding and pointedly reveals that the first derivative of c (speed of light) is one or unity! Since net exchanges of EADs equal 0, J = 0. But, there is need to consider the perihelion advance of Mercury resulting from a loss of J "to the greater universe".

Mapping of Maxwell's equations with the "Particle Electro-Dynamics" (PED) of EADs of gravity completes this confirmation of Albert Einstein's "Unified Field Theory", preferably called "The Unified Field Theory of 'Charged Particle' Relations and Mass-Energy Transformation(s)", with "mathematical rigor" as a unified view of the greater universe. Einstein did not require that atomic theory be a part of his "unified field". But, when the "particle" phenomena are recognized to result from "mutual atomic-molecular polarity(ies)", unity of gravity and electromagnetism unites the atomic theory also.

Another paragraph regarding "mathematical rigor" seems necessary. The idea that mathematics is a "pure science" is consistent with this author's position that "reasonable and informed people can resolve perceptual inversions" (or disagreements) about "physical reality and find its' mathematical description" and then make that description perceptual reality for "all reasonable people". In the course of this author's study of mathematics regarding the matter of the "unified field" he has found many mathematical theorists. There is a mathematical school of thought called Brouwer's "Intuition of the Integers" that denies the reality of "step functions" like the known, real matter-energy transformation and its quantum unit h, Planck's constant. This paper supports the Platonist theory of mathematics that contains the "Law of the Excluded Middle", projecting as fact that mass ($|X|$) is not energy ($|-X|$), but is energy transformed. X is 7.372×10^{-51} kg, EAD1m. -X is 6.626×10^{-34} Joules, EAD1e. ^{X}and $^{-X}$ are complements with 90-degree parity. EAD1m is attached to an AMD (receptor) and associated with an electron hole 90 degrees away. EAD1e has $v = c$ and leaves an open AMD (receptor) site, closing an electron hole in the valence layer (band). EAD1e and EAD1m are different real states of energy or mass (matter), respectfully, -X and X. To suggest that Brouwer was right in his perception of human perception, but not right in his perception of mathematics as the "pure science" is best illustrated with a second example. The first example, already given, is that mass-energy transformation has real quantum changes of fixed unit "particles". The second example is the story of "Ted" Williams' visual perception as different from the "normal" baseball player's. It is said that "Ted" could see the blank spaces between pictures projected onto motion picture screens during movies so that he could not go to the movies without getting a headache. But this visual "frequency perception" acuity or time related perceptual reality, while painful at the movies, is what may have been an edge in hitting a baseball, for he could also see each thread of the baseball as it approached him from the pitchers. Presented above are two physical phenomena and their perception(s) by different persons. Phenomena described in Platonist terms are less subjective than human perceptual reality as reflected by Brouwer's and "Ted" Williams' abilities. The "split" of perceptual reality of witnesses "splits" them into two perceptual inclination "sets" as: 1) Intuitive between the integers (Brouwer) or

2) Platonist with reality oriented "excluded middles"("Ted" Williams). This paper suggests Planck's constant has energy reality with integer frequency minus one through minus infinity for energy as a "step function" with "excluded middles" between integers. It also maintains Planck's constant has reality use in electron orbits or "energy levels" but suggests they are better recognized as mass quantum

additions or losses to atommolecules. Further, Planck's constant has reality with "frequency" or quanta one through perceptual infinity as whole integers with "excluded middles" between integers for mass as an "associate" complement "element" of energy, better perceived as a positive state for mass, due to the convention of assigning the negative sign to an electron. Finally, Planck's constant is recognized in this paper to result from the limit of v (velocity) for all real "particles" to c (the speed of light), so that it is the result of the limit of an electron's energy as a particle that determines Planck's constant as a function of energy-time or energy/frequency. Planck's constant is the natural parity of the property of c (speed of light) having a derivative of one or $dx/dt = dt/dx = 1$. The limit of c (speed of light) for "particles" is a real and true finding of Albert Einstein.

The core belief of Albert Einstein was that a "unified field" of physics could be described by "one formula". This paper agrees with that core belief and suggests that perception becomes a true and non-"general"[32] (non-random) reality by "pure mathematics" unencumbered by "subjective" "intuition of the integers" of Brouwerian mathematics characteristic of Riemannian-Gaussian integration. The future of physics, our common perception of the universe, and our physical ability to deal with it, depends upon our approach to perception and action. Are we to have an "Intuition of the Integers" by mystical, defined perception of "particles" and "waves" or are we to have reality-oriented, Platonist perception of "kernel elements" that lead us to associative fusion, rather than a string or transform of dissociative, but quantitative, thoughts. The choice is between an intuitive "fantasy of brilliance" and actually finding the truth, definition or discovery. This paper suggests real "kernel elements" as the proper origin for discovery.

References for Chapter VIII:

1 Clark, Ronald (1971, 1984), **EINSTEIN – The Life and Times** (P. 495). Avon Books, An Imprint of Harper and Collins Publishers, 10 East 53rd Street, N.Y., N.Y.

2 McHenry, Robert, General Editor, **The New Encyclopaedia Britannica** 15th Edition, 1992. Vol. 23 P. 768. Chicago, Illinois.
3 Ibid. 2.

4 Ibid 1 P. 771.

5 Ibid 2 Vol. 13, P. 294.

6 Lodge, Oliver (Sir). **The Ether Space**. Source: Ibid 1, Pp. 298-299.

7 "Mass changes space about it." Source: Zitzewitz, Paul W. Neff, Robert F. Davids, Mark (1995). Merrill **Physics Principles and Problems** P. 169. Glencoe/McGraw-Hill N.Y., N.Y.

8 *Nature*, October 9, 1975 quote from de Sitter letter.

9 Ibid 7.

10 Miller, Franklin, Jr. (1959). **College Physics** Pp 105-106. Brace and World and Company, Inc., New York.

11 Piaget, Jean (1937), "Principle Factors Determining Intellectual Evolution From Childhood to Adult Life", from Rapaport, David (1951, 1956, 1959), **ORGANIZATION AND PATHOLOGY OF THOUGHT**: Selected Sources, Pp. 154-192. Columbia University Press, N.Y. Also from: Factors Determining Human Behavior: Harvard Tercentenary Conference of Arts and Sciences, by Edgar Douglas Adrain, et al., Cambridge Mass.: Harvard University Press, Copyright 1937 by the President and Fellows of Harvard College.

12 Ibid 5.

13 Ibid 5.

14 Ibid 5.

15 Ibid 5.

16 Ibid 5.

17 Ibid 5.

18 Ibid 5.

19 "Transforms" and "renormalization" result from failure to "identify" the very real "kernel element" but in truthful quantitative determinations, if states are preserved. The author's favored source of their use is: Einstein, Albert (1905). "*On The Electrodynamics Of Moving Bodies*". Annalen der Physic 17: 891-921.

20 Kernberg, Otto F., M.D. **Borderline Conditions and Pathological Narcissism**, Pp. 29-34, 229, 264, 265, 269. Jason Aronson, Inc. Northvale, N.J. and London, England.

21 Ibid 19.

22 Ibid 2 V. 23 Pp. 554-555.

23 Ibid 1, P. 157.

24 Ibid 7, P. 558.

25 Pauling's "no danger of confusion". Pauling, Linus (1935, 1963). **Introduction to Quantum Mechanics With Applications to Chemistry** (428-436). General Publishing Company, Ltd. 30 Lesmill Road, Don Mills, Toronto, Ontario, Canada.

26 Ibid 2, V. 23, Pp. 554-555.

27 Davis, Frank E., III., M.D. (2005-2006) "Psychoanalysis: Seeing Through the 'Reality Principle' To Find Psychical Reality For the Narcissistic Personality Disorders".

28 Ibid 7.

29 Ibid 8.

30 Ibid 1, P. 772.

31 Ibid 2, V. 7, P. 968-969.

32 Ibid 25, Pp. 398-399.

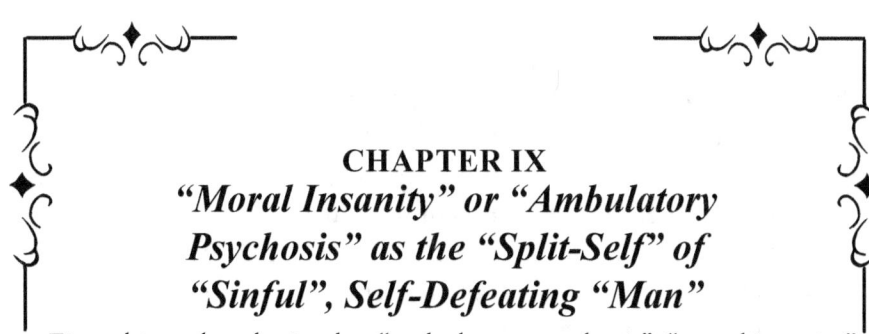

CHAPTER IX
"Moral Insanity" or "Ambulatory Psychosis" as the "Split-Self" of "Sinful", Self-Defeating "Man"

First, this author denies that "ambulatory psychosis", "moral insanity", the "Oedipal complex", or the "split-self" is always present in everyone. That stance is evil's denial of "truth", as a real state, at any time, for anyone. But, what is that "evil," "split self"? It is best understood using Dostoyevsky's view in *"Crime and Punishment"* when he says that "moral insanity" is that split state of consciousness where one feels one has "a more noble purpose than the law" in one's conscious mind, but in one's subconscious, preconscious, or unconscious mind that same (split) person has, as his/her "motive, power or money for himself". So that, each time the written law is violated, the "split", "morally insane" "self" is said to exist.

Using Dostoyevsky's model of "moral insanity", each time the U.S. Supreme Court makes a decision of "more noble purpose than (written) law" (constitution) they (the justices) exhibit "moral insanity". Likewise, each time the "normal scientist" fails to admit to and correct untruthfulness or duplicity in his science, he exhibits the "moral insanity" or "ambulatory psychosis" that he is in control of the truth. In the "exhibition" of this "moral insanity" or "ambulatory psychosis" he/she proves that he/she is not in control of truth, but often "projects" that others are not in control of that "truth" or that "truth" is "unknowable" or can "never be found, never".

This chapter takes the position that submission of the self to prior established law or science is necessary to avoid "moral insanity" exhibition unless one can demonstrate duplicity (untruthfulness) in that law or science or its general interpretation. Because this author explicitly demonstrates duplicity of thought as the present practices of the "normal sciences" of psychoanalysis and physics and demonstrates the association of those practices with states of consciousness related to the "superego-ego complex", he believes this book to be very valuable to all persons seeking truthfulness or the reality state of life. The truth test of the practitioners of the "normal sciences" of psychoanalysis and physics, as to process of thought, is presented by the behavior of the editors of their journals. The "process" of the other practitioners of these "normal sciences" will be determined by whether they truthfully answer the questions raised as "the need(s) of the situation" and show evidence of problem solution or merely attack this author with "negativity". This author awaits the reaction(s) of the readers and the "normal scientists" with peaceful joy and Einstein's wry smile.

The rules of "fair play" in science are that a theory or theories must be recognized and challenged until proven as law or proven to be misrepresentations of reality. Since the theories that: 1) "The fantasy worlds and false beliefs of the personality disorders are the superego identifiers of persons with those disorders"; 2) "The EAD, as completely identified, is the unity element of the 'unified field' theory and gives the 'strings' suggested by 'string theory'", are theories currently not challenged or addressed explicitly, they should be recognized, by all persons of "fair play" as working principles that "answer the needs of the situation"(s). "Fair play" requires the "kings" of these "normal science" "kingdoms" to, explicitly and consciously, disprove these theories or give up their "kingdoms". This author is not trying to be a "giant killer", but he is suggesting that they are "not meeting the needs of the situation"(s) and he is publicly "calling them out" (see below for more detail) to meet the responsibility(ies) of their well-compensated positions!

"Moral insanity", when understood to violate the broader law of the greater universe of truth of the "selfevident" fact that "all men are created equal", is recognized as "identifiable" with "the aggressor states" of all personality disorders. When "identification with the aggressor states" or "fantasy worlds" is recognized as the core nature of all personality disorders, the "golden rule" of "Do unto others as you would have them do unto you", or consciousness of true self and true others, is recognized as the healthy personality. Lack of this healthy "state of consciousness" is then recognized to result from failure to "identify" the "self" with the non-aggressor, truthful, loving state (as a superego value identifier) of awareness of the "others".

The psychoanalysts have well-identified knowledge of faulty "self and object images", in others, with the six personality disorders associated with the unreal fantasy worlds of "brilliance, unlimited power, unlimited wealth, unlimited fame, ideal or unlimited love, and unequaled beauty. Examples of those with the fantasy of brilliance have been demonstrated. An example of the fantasy of unlimited wealth is the self-destructiveness of some great prize-fighters (and other great athletes) who have earned enormous amounts of money, yet wound up "broke" due to spending in excess of very large, but not unlimited, incomes. Adolph Hitler is an example of a personality who lived in the fantasy world of unlimited fame or power. Those who expect "ideal" or unlimited "love", without giving love in return, deny the real limits of their objects and "over-idealize" themselves as lovable spirits. Those, like the queen, step-mother, in "***Snow White***", who live in the fantasy world of unequaled beauty are in denial of the reality of others, like Snow White, and have the "aggressor state" as to "self" as an unreal person of unequaled-beauty. Each fantasy world of the narcissistic personality disorders, and each false belief of the other personality disorders, can be shown to be self-defeating, just as this book shows the fantasy world of brilliance or "knowing", as a "self" "identification", to be self-defeating. For the emotionally perceptive, these disorders are recognized to result from re-projection of primary relationships.

It is his perception of the emotional pain associated with the "split" of "self" that occurs with the personality disorders, as well as the nature of their origins, that gives this author empathy for persons with these disorders. Their pain is related to his pain when he finds himself, or them, to be untruthful. Yet, truthfulness is his "ideal self" and, because it is not universal in him or the world, is also an "ideal self" that is emotionally "splitting". Yet, truthfulness is not destructive of the "true self" or the truth of others and it does not deny reality. Personalities perceptually living in the fantasy worlds of "moral insanity", by identifying themselves with "aggressor states" destroy their perception of their real life and usually "project" that destruction upon the behavior of others. It is actually their own negative behavior(s) and perception(s) that destroy(s) them, all resulting from a "false alliance" of "self" with negative reality as a core value.

The term "calling them out" might allude most readers to western movies where the villain calls his opposite to a gunfight in the public street. This makes it a "bombshell" term likely to receive attention.

The attention this author seeks is, not towards himself, but is to attempt to get the reading public to force the editors of the journals of these "normal sciences" and "normal scientists", who view themselves as physicists or psychoanalysts, to focus their consciousness on the question(s) as to truthfulness (+) or falseness (-) of the two theses that: 1) "The superego identifier of persons with personality disorders is the fantasy world or false belief of those disorders"; and 2) "The unity element of the 'unified field' or 'Grand Unified Theory' (GUT)is the EAD1c as completely identified in this book which results in recognition of the 'strings' or associative linkages of 'String Theory'". The truthfulness of each of these two theses does not relate this author to each party "called out" but relates to the truthfulness or falseness of their own personal perceptual position on the theses. **Their** personal perceptual position, clearly, should not relate to that of this author, as **they** are the experts of these respective fields. The term "calling them out" does not relate to a contest with this author, but attempts to bring general consciousness to the fact that these editors, and all the "normal scientists" of these two "normal sciences", must either answer the questions of these two theses or consciously admit they "do not know" the answer to the core questions of their "normal science". Of course, answer to the big questions requires answers to smaller "details" (Einstein's term), like, "Is $E = Mc^2$ or $-E = Mc^2$?" and, "Since the psycho-analysts assume the position of "object" in psychoanalysis, and the object, by "transference", becomes the primary object, how do analysts keep themselves and the primary object separate in their analytic processes, so that the ego and superego of patients are both 'identified'?" and; "How do analysts separate the ego (as id, primitive ego, or soul) and superego-ego complex of patients?" Readers should recognize this author wants no relationship to the editors or "normal scientists" of these scientific disciplines, except one of truthfulness as relates to the true or false conceptualizations of the core of their "science". This position of the author raises several questions that he would like to present to the reading public:

1. Are these editors and "normal scientists" able to separate themselves, and this author, from the "state of knowing" or "science" or is their consciousness tied inextricably with their own "state of knowing"?

2. Can they see "science", as Einstein did, as a "reality apart from humanity", or is their "reality" "self"?

3. Do they have the ability to see that "self" may be untruthful and presented as real?

4. To phrase this in Biblical terms, can they separate themselves from "original sin"?

5. Can they find a truth that is separate from their emotional self or is their "truth" that "self" is truth (or reality)?

6. If their belief is that "self" is truth, do they occasionally separate "self" from truth?

Einstein said, "I cannot prove that scientific truth must be conceived as a truth that is valid independent of 'reality', but I believe it firmly... Our natural point of view in regard to the existence of truth apart from humanity cannot be explained or proved. But it is a belief which nobody can lack-not primitive beings even. We attribute to truth a superhuman objectivity, it is indispensable for us, this reality which is independent of our mindthough we cannot say what it means".1 This quote comes from Clark's **EINSTEIN**- *The Life and Times* (P. 504). The single quote marks about the word "reality" are this author's. Recognize that Einstein is not distinguishing between his own personal perception and "reality", therefore, to those truly in the know that "perception is not necessarily reality", his words prove themselves to be truthful. To those oriented to the true fact that "perception is not necessarily reality", Einstein's words are truthful on their face. But, his words also exhibit his own perception of "self" as a personality-in-action who believes his perception is "reality" or "truth", and believes himself to be "brilliant" or able "to know" "reality", implicitly or intuitively.

Jesus, the Christ, of Nazareth said, (John 14: 6), to Thomas, "I am the way, the truth, and the life: no man cometh unto the Father, but by me." (John 14: 14), "Even the Spirit of truth; whom the world cannot receive, because it seeth him not, neither knoweth him: but ye know him; for he dwelleth with you and shall be in you." In these verses of John 14, a man called Jesus and born in Nazareth relates that he is truth and is separate from the world (or then current world view). His "self" identifier is "truth". He says that truth separates Himself from Einstein's humanity (the world view of humanity) and is the way to

God (omnipotence). Other verses say that Jesus said that "truth" is "life" and that a worldly view of self and others is death.

Truthfulness is the "splitting" agent of "moral sanity" and reality that separates those who are alive from those who exhibit "ambulatory psychosis". It is found by recognizing and avoiding duplicity or resolving its presence, not by denial of its' existence. This author chooses to "identify" himself with truthfulness, as an ego ideal, and to suggest that such an ego ideal is "the path less traveled", but, in the broader view, that ego ideal was given to him by his mother as the "core value" of their relationship(s).

CHAPTER X
Finding the "Lost" Soul of a Person and Finding the True Spirit of a Personality

There is "Confusion of Tongues"1in discussions about spirituality. Present psychoanalytic persons either do not use terms like superego and primitive ego in their thought or they seem to be applying them improperly, as presented above. Chapter X presents the finding that those in the mental health profession appear to be unable to perceive the superego and primitive ego as separate from the ego. Again, the reason appears to be because of their inability to perceive anything beyond "a direct visible truth"2. This is Dr. Sheldon Bach's narcissistic state of consciousness3, but it is directed to the analysts, instead of their patients. The second chapter of Part I presented this view, but this chapter reveals the historical "equalities" of words used in the religious or spiritual community with those of the professional mental health analysts, as used in their literature, as opposed to their apparent practice. This is presented in tabular form: Superego Parent(s), Ideal Self, Value system. This is what spiritual people call the "spirit" of a person. Computer people might call the superego the software, operating system. Ego Self-image or "self". Primitive Ego a part of the Id This is the "soul" before it is contaminated by "worldly" experience and the conceptualization of that experience by false words or misalliances. The soul is as pure as mathematics, until it becomes contaminated by "worldly" events or the false conceptualization of them. It is associated with the physical body of the new- born baby and the genes of the chromosomes unrelated to worldly contamination or untruthful conceptualization. Id stands for the "it". Physical and genetic person without "worldly" experience. Narcissism, Personality Disorders. Persons with behavioral problems consistent with "sin" or "selfishness". These are "Sinful Man (or woman)" syndromes and they are real patterns of behavior described in the DSM criteria. "Transference" This is a recognized phenomenon that children learn how to behave as disciples of those who are responsible for them in a process called discipline. Responsibility and discipline can be absent in the primary relationship and result in their absence in future relationships of the child(ren). All present and absent characteristics of the parent(s) can be "transferred" to the child(ren) in the process called "identification". Chapter Two presented the failure of analysts to use this phenomenon as due to narcissism. This can be thought of as the "compulsion to associate" other persons with the primary relationship or primary caretaker. If the primary caretaker was untruthful in word or dead, it is a "compulsion to associate" untruthfully. Fantasy This is a daydream. Fantasy World This is Chuck Colson's[4] "world view". It is interesting that this author used that term, "world view", independently of Mr. Colson's reference to it, in his first "paper" on these disorders. It is the person's value system with "identities" for "self" and "object"(s). Because it "identifies" both the value system and the object, it is presented in this book as an "identity" with superego and "self", ego. Denial This is perceived as a lie. It is actually a false statement and thought to protect a false "self" or to protect "self" from an unbearable truth like a natural disaster or threatening situation. See the three types of Denial in chapter Two. Repression Complete failure to make near obvious associations, usually due to a history of a severely traumatic event. "Material" Matters of fact associated with emotionally charged patient (or analyst's) perceptual reality (interpretations). "Regression" Patient's given history, obtained through the technique of "free association" or hypnosis, which reaches primeval scenes of childhood. Also, to go back in developmental history (enabling dissociation of false associations or misalliances). "Interpretation" The analyst's association of the regression with the oedipal complex (hate) or dissociation of the patient's true emotions from the false superego by application of "transference" (love) due to true "identification" of the patient's real situation (love) as opposed to that of the analyst.

Present "spirit" of Freudian psychoanalysis = The Oedipal complex. This is the totem and taboo of Freud. It is the hate, envy, lies, and murder of the father by his sons and similar alleged feelings of the daughters for the mother. It is "empty" of perception of the positive relationships that can exist between parents and children. It does represent a portion of the "real" relationships, unfortunately. This is a "negative", "mirror"-image of the true spiritual life. It was felt by Freud to be universally applicable. It lacks synthesis of worldly and spiritual perceptions, because it has no spiritual (emotional) perception. Thus, it is a perception limited to worldly truths that falsely projects those worldly truths to "unworldly" people, such as true Christians and other generally truthful persons. While Freud saw the totem and taboo related to Christian communion, he did not recognize the Christian value of a love and life-giving father, shown by his son whose shed blood is life and whose sacrificed body is shed in truth.

The Soul of Psychoanalysis: "Transference" or Freud's "identification" process with the primary object. "Transference" projected to a truthful person exhibits the true "spirit" of the personality in question and reveals the loving or hating "spirit" of that personality's primary caretaker. A true perception of a "spirit" reveals a loving or hating "spirit" that is the real global personality. True Christians, unlike Freudians, always view the soul of a person as loving and looking for love. The provable "instinct" is the tendency towards unity. This is made especially clear by an understanding of Freud and Breuer's recognition of the "compulsion to associate", even dissociated material. THE IDENTITY EQUATION OF PSYCHOANALYSIS IS: World view = Superego-ego Complex

It is explained as: projected perception and behavior result from the parent to child relationship, which can be negative as well as positive. The more true associations we, as parents or scientists, can convey to our children, the better we leave them. The fewer false associations, we as parents or scientists, pass on to them, the better off they are. Denial of true associations, for any reason, is harmful. Promotion of false associations is just as harmful. Rigidity is inability to learn from history perceived in a truthful way. Denial of truth as reality has as its motive egocentrism, selfishness, or sin. "Unknowable" is often laziness, by another word.

The table above is provided for the spiritual reader to be able to make associations that might not be obvious because of lack of exposure to them. The rest of Chapter X is dedicated to demonstrating some "REAL" entities that you probably have already perceived, but have not had names to "identify" them with. The purpose of this Chapter X is to assist you in your verbal and intellectual "defense" of your faith or spiritual perceptions and subsequent "feelings" or emotions, when they are challenged.

The perceptual reality of an all-powerful God, an earthly prophet or savior, and an invisible "spirit", has a true "logic of relations" to "real" concepts of the mental health professionals and "real" entities of our physical world. If you will just review the table, you will see that the soul and spirits are "real" concepts in the mental health literature. Many mental health professionals seem to enter the profession in order to "find themselves". This is at least a partial reason why this profession seems to have so much denial of their own literature and spirituality. These professionals with responsibility to be "role models" for good mental health are unable to assist those who need help precisely because of their lack of spiritual perception as related to their own repression. The "world view" they perceive and present, in their "therapies" and papers of their journals, needs to be challenged just as this book challenges "the Heisenberg uncertainty principle". Their "world view" is provable as fantasy, just as the "transformation equations" are shown to defend errantly interpreted scientific data perception by inverting it. Persons, who deny spirituality, love, and emotional perception, have "real" deficits in their perceptual awareness and state of consciousness. Their spirits are negative and untrue, due to fantasy worlds or false beliefs, and their perception is limited to these fantasy worlds and boring. We, the believers, must love their souls and seek to help them with their spirits. We should know the very positive "magnificent feeling" we get when we are in harmony with nature comes from our "identification" with truthfulness or unity of thought with nature. We may be able to lead those with negative personalities to happiness, if we can show them love while relating their errant thought to their past. Recognizing this errant thought and these personality disorder syndromes will help us in the strength of our faith. We must not allow negative personalities to simply suggest we are "rigid" when we stand up for truthfulness, as they simply stand for a "Self" of fantasy. Life is most exciting when we seek the truth about our objects, our world, and ourselves. Truthfulness is the way to a happy and productive life. Think of the equation:

(For the atom(s)): $\Delta^{Mc2} = \Delta E = EADn \times -EADe = EADn \times EADm \times c^2 = EADn \times +/-EADc$ at velocity c (dependent upon direction + towards a specific mass or position in question) = (For Gravity): $1/2(G((M1M2/d1^2)$

+ (M1$_\Delta$M2$_\Delta$/d2^2))) x Δd = (For Electromagnetism): 1/2(K((q1q^2/d12) + (q1$_\Delta$q2$_\Delta$/d2^2))) x Δd $^{\text{For Gravity and Electromagnetism}}$ Δd is positive when decreasing. Perception of the EAD1as a "particle" is intuitively apparent when thought of as "mass" or "charge". But when the EAD1is thought of as energy, it is intuitively perceived as a "wave", even though it is only one "particle" E is God, the all-powerful, maker of heaven and earth. M was the physical body of the savior and continues to be the body of matter associated with truth. The analysts call this verbal matter, "material". Do not ever let persons with repression deny you the reality of real, physically demonstrable truth. Work hard to find it. Each and every EAD is real physical energy of a kind that can be positive, like a Holy Spirit. Of course there are negatives of all of these! The prince of the world, Satan, needs recognition, just as the ruler of the universe.

A theme of this book is that untruth is spotted by perception of duplicity. The complement of that is that, truth is found by proving the negative of duplicity or proving the absence of duplicity. While the reader may perceive this book as "negative", if the reader is duplicitous, exposure of the reader to his own duplicity, could be the cause of perception of "negativity", even if that exposure of self of reader is subconscious. What we do not want is tolerance of true "negativity", as to spiritual perception, in any of us, and that includes you and me! To follow the false spiritual path, even if it is easier, more profitable in the short run, or superficially more "tolerant", is to deny our selves reality in our living! In the long run, this author can prove every selfish or narcissistic trait to be self-defeating. This book should, unequivocally, show every reader that there are absolute truths, but they can only be found with synthesis or consistency of self with emotion and interest perceptions in harmony.

Recognizing the two states of consciousness to relate to the brain as a functioning unit, (1) The interest or left cerebral hemisphere of the brain and the (2) Libidinal or emotional right cerebral hemisphere, allows us to see that duplicity results from a "split" brain, as well as an overtly "split" self. To avoid evil in others and our selves we must learn how to recognize these splits in perception. It should be especially comforting to Christians to recognize the familiar "Golden Rule" as the way to avoid evil in personal and scientific perception. That is, in perception, personal and scientific, use due care to make truthful "identifications". This author likes useful and true labels. One label is an "instrument of perception". The "Golden Rule" is just such an instrument. Another is the three criteria of Masters and Johnson5 for recognizing "Commitment". (1) A willingness to make one's self vulnerable to the other party (object). (2) Truthfulness to one's self. (3) Truthfulness to one's partner. This love and true "Walking in the Spirit" of Christ is not self-sacrificing. It is self-fulfilling, because it is true to the soul or true self. The problem is that so many people have an interest self that is not true to the soul or true self! Guess how they got it? You're RIGHT! "IDENTIFICATION" with a person with a false spirit. Now, to say something Christians might not like. The most difficult part of this book is to present to people, who believe themselves to be truthful, the real difficulty involved in actually fulfilling that self-image and its unimaginable benefits. For over a month, this author has struggled with the problem of how to project this Christian reality of "truth" to non-Christians without their perceiving aggression from the Christian or Christ "identity". The first approach, maintained until today (2-01-06), was to deny the use of the name "Jesus" and promote the "truth" "identity". This approach, even with a "superficial" Christian assessment, set the author up as having "truth" within his own perception of "duplicity" and denied the truth of Jesus and the "identity" of his name and life (truth). The word is "truth" and it is life. John 6: 63, "the words that I speak unto you, they are spirit, and they are life". So, going to the word, it is recognized that the truthful (Christian) life requires a double burden on us in our perceptual process to realize the unimaginable benefits that result from finding truth. Reality is in seeking, not "knowing". The double burden is found in this struggle to find peace for self without denial of our object (Jesus and all other people he wants us to relate to). It is projected in the words of Matthew 10: 38-39, "He that taketh not his cross, and followeth after me, is not worthy of me. He that findeth his life shall lose it: and he that loseth his life for my sake shall find it." This correlates with the state of "knowing" as sin or denial of truth (Christ). To avoid denial of truth (Jesus), we must deny our self the assumption of "knowing" and perfection. To avoid denial of our objects (usually in our subconscious), we must deny our self-expectations of full knowledge or perfection from them. By seeking truth (Jesus and our other real objects) we find it; we find real life. True behavior is not disadvantageous, compromising, or political. Truthful behavior is self- actualization. The loss of worldly self is the birth of real self and the beginning of real life. Only truthful knowledge has real power. It is the truth of the spirit or finding the soul that is love of self and other. But, it may be impossible to do anything more than recognize a "split" world of evil negativism and real positive truths. Truth of behavior then becomes recognition of the realities of evil and good as thought and behavior in opposite directions, with evil as self-defeating. "Identities" Remember true "identities" are not exclusive of each other, where false "identities" "deny" or "repress" reality:

Jesus=Truth=Love=interdependence=good feelings=positive life=happiness= Perception of Good and Evil only with Truthfulness Satan=Hate=Lies=dependence (subconscious)=Autism (conscious)=fear=envy=unhappiness Denial of Evil in Self, Denial of Good in Others John 6: 63: "the words that I speak unto you, they are spirit, and they are life." Mathew 16: 26 "For what is a man profited, if he should gain the whole world, and lose his own soul? Or what shall a man give in exchange for his soul? Answer: His life is lost with the loss of truth.

Remember equivalence as an "identity" and every time you meet a person, with a known soul, think of them as Jesus or your savior. Show the love of your true soul for unity with theirs. Find the truth of their spirit (whether it be false or true) and truth for yours. You then have two "identities". Because of the imperfection of "worldly" people neither will be Jesus as to behavior, but can become so, as to thought, and maybe later, as to behavior. When that unity is achieved, both parties have Einstein's "magnificent feeling". Now, you are left to your own "free will". When you have love of truth you will have love of soul, true self.

References to Chapter X:

1 Ferenzi, Sandor (1932). Confusion of Tongues Between Adults and the Child. Paper presented at the International Psychoanalytic Congress, September 1932, in Wiesbaden. IJP, 1949. Translation in: Masson's, Jeffrey (1984, 1985). THE ASSAULT ON TRUTH —

Freud's Suppression of the Seduction Theory, Pp. 291-302. Penguin Books, Viking Penguin, Inc.

2 Clark, Ronald (1971, 1984), **EINSTEIN** – The Life and Times (P. 284-289). Avon Books, An Imprint of Harper and Collins Publishers, 10 East 53rd Street, N.Y., N.Y.

3 Bach, Sheldon. (1977). "On the Narcissistic State of Consciousness". International Journal of Psychoanalysis 58: 209-233.

4 Colson, Charles (1999). **The Problem of Evil** (introduction). Tyndale House Publishers, Inc. Wheaton, Illinois.

5 Masters, William H. Johnson, Virginia E. Levin, Robert J. (1970, 1971, 1972, 1973, 1974). **The Pleasure Bond.** Bantam Books, Inc. 666 Fifth Avenue, N.Y., N.Y., 10019.

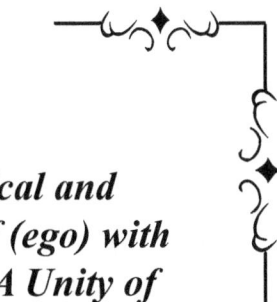

CHAPTER XI
"Integration" of the Physical and Spiritual Universe Or the Self (ego) with the Soul (primitive ego of id A Unity of the Physical and Social Sciences

It has been difficult for the author to keep the four entities of consciousness of the physical and social sciences apart in the previous presentations. This is usually true for some people, because of "free association" and "free conceptual construction". But for others, such associations are "loose associations", because they must keep their emotions and interests separate or "split". They "feel" they must keep the emotional mind separate from reality because of repression. This is the cause of the split. There is a true relationship between MatterEnergy and the Conscious-Subconscious. Let's take a trip that will be fantasy for some.

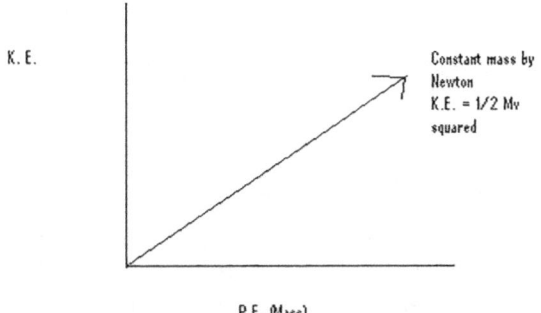

P.E. (Mass)

(1) If you view the kinetic energy versus velocity²graph: (a) Kinetic energy (K.E.) versus velocity squared (v2) at constant mass with proper units has a 45-degree slope. (b) Notice that K.E. for v. in this classical manner of constant mass is: $K.E. = 1/2Mv^2$.

(c) But, for M at c (the velocity of light and other electromagnetic waves), where c is the upper limit of v: $E = -(Mc^2)$, because M is totally consumed in that interval at that velocity (c). It all becomes electromagnetic energy or K.E. (d) Now for all universes: K.E. + P.E. (Potential Energy, mass) = Total energy. So, for all universes with mass, a graph can be constructed such that, as P.E. increases K.E. decreases, or as mass increases energy decreases. Realize now, we are talking "transformation" or change of state from K.E. to P.E. (energy to mass). (e) The "equilibrium mass" is 1/2of the total and is the 45 degree slope perpendicular to the line graphed for K.E. versus P.E. The "Ideal" or "Equilibrium Mass" appears to be a naturally existing "Ideal"! "Equilibrium mass" is the mass of potential energy, as opposed to energy at c, for a given temperature and pressure.

(2) Now to make the big leap! Recognize that the "Ideal" state of consciousness is precisely in the "Preconscious" where decisions are made by superego "fit" or "shape" described by Sandler and others[1,2]. So that the "Ideal" or "Equilibrium State" of consciousness is the "preconscious mind" where conscious "Self" and subconscious "Object" are equally conscious and subconscious. The best "preconscious mind" appears to have a "real" slope of forty-five degrees on the graph of "Conscious self" versus "Subconscious object". This is the "Ideal state of the preconscious" for all times and places. It is the "decision-making time" or the "Time of Truth" or the time of "Free Will"! Now, recognize this as the conscious state of Jesus Christ! Remember He said, "I am the way, the 'truth', and the life"? This was His defined ego!He knew God loved him and he was to be the "body of truth". Has the reader recognized this as an "identity", "identification" or "mathematical identity"?

Let's attempt an identity equation of Christ's concept: Christ = Truth = "Ideal Self" = "Preconscious" = "Free will" = true decisions relative to "real" situations. Does anyone deny Jesus Christ as a "real" person who said the words above? This "identity" of the line of truth was presented to the author as "the chalk line" when he was a child and is recognized by all Christians as "walking in the spirit". Others recognize this truthful approach to life and use words like "stand up guy", "up and flying right", etc. The gray, shaded area is all decisions of the preconscious biased to the self. This is a "grandiose self". The black area is biased to the object and is the "devalued self". A grandiose self results in a devalued object and vice versa. The terms or "identifiers," "walking the chalk line" and "walking in the spirit" are identified sufficiently to be put in the "identity equation", above. A graph can be drawn to illustrate truth as a preconscious standard that is a real entity where, truthful consciousness of object, equals truthful consciousness of self. This does not imply that truthful consciousness is affected by biased perception from self or object. Truthful perception demands truthful description of the real situation (a real "identification") unaffected by prior emotional (libidinal) history. "Conscious self" Truth "Unconscious object"

This graph has the same appearance as the K.E. versus P.E. graph, where "Ideal Mass" is the forty-five degree slope and it is perpendicular to the graph line of the mathematical relationship of K.E. versus P.E. for all total "Equivalent Masses". But, in this graph, the "Y" axis is "Conscious self" and the "X" axis is "Subconscious object". All "states of consciousness" for a given bit of "material" or situation are the area below the line perpendicular to the "Ideal Preconscious" of "Truth". These entities are known to be "real" graph able situations! Of course, they have previously been spiritually perceived. This conceptualization is the "Golden Rule": Matthew 7: 12: Jesus speaking, "Therefore of all things whatsoever you would that men should do to you, do ye even so to them: for this is the law and the prophets." This is the "Magnificent Feeling" of Einstein. It is also the "Oceanic Feeling"[3,4] written about by Rolland and taken up by Freud, a feeling he did not have as an adult. This "Oceanic Feeling" cannot be underestimated. It is the emotional equivalent of what heaven is said to be. It is physical and spiritual synthesis of perception of unimaginable intensity and productivity. It is love and truth integrated into unity. The "grandiose self" is to the left of "Ideal" of the truth of preconscious, and is towards "Conscious self". The projected self of Sigmund Freud is the grandiose self. The "devalued self" is to the right of the "Ideal Preconscious" of truth and is towards the "Subconscious object". This "devalued self" was the state of consciousness for Albert Einstein. Since gain of self is loss of object, just as loss of self (from devaluation) is a gain of object, they are unrelated and an inverse relationship destructive of unity. To force relatedness is therefore a "compulsion to associate" the dissociated or a transference, mésalliance, or false association. The forty-five degree line between conscious and subconscious is the state of consciousness of a truthful person. Now the author has believed, for a long time, someone should give the "states of consciousness" attention. Before doing so, Bach's good "paper"[5], as a descriptive work, requires a criticism. , as a descriptive work, requires a criticism. 221), their superegos. This is, of course, Bach's denial of the superego as a real factor in the mental processes of real persons. A superego that prejudices one to current reality is a force that has been taken into the self that controls self as to perception, inhibiting perception of the true current situation. It is improper for an analyst to deny real intra-psychic phenomena related to psychic energies or cathexes. Bach expresses a "lack of empathy" and exhibits Einstein's "positivistic philosophic attitude", as well as denial of superego functions, when he says, (Pp. 213-214), "When a patient says that he is 'falling apart', feels 'like two people', has 'no willpower', no 'identity', or feels that his body 'is in pieces', we are under no compulsion to translate this directly and anthropomorphically into its (apparent) metapsychologically structural equivalent". This statement exhibits lack of empathy for both the patients' expressed psychic dysfunction and the given rationale for how psychoanalysis works, through regression and synthesis. Maybe more revealing, it shows that Bach's "positivistic philosophic attitude" results from his grandiose confidence that he is "knowing" or "brilliant" by clear description, alone, without the synthesis that comes from recognition that a fantasy world, as a faulty conceptualization of reality by superego (parent), causes all the symptoms as merely described by Bach, without this synthesis. This author will now discuss six states of consciousness:

(1) Fantasy is a loss of clarity of present conscious self and/or object images with intact sensory-motor capacity due to a daydream focus of consciousness. Without rigid, untruthful or impossible identities for self and/or objects, fantasy can be a useful vision or "free conceptual construction". (2) A near total loss of true, self and object images with sensory-motor orientation to person, place, and time is the antisocial personality. This is the "pure culture" of narcissism. It is a "lost" or "split" self due to a fantasy world, such as the fantasy world of unlimited wealth, power. (3) Schizophrenia is associated with the four "As" of Bleuler and is a near total loss of touch with "reality". This author believes it, to result from a "split" of "self" into two irreconcilable superegos. It is often not a constant state and appears to occur coincident with stress. It is often associated with auditory voices inconsistent with visual reality. Paranoia and other "personality" pathologies are often associated with schizophrenia. (4) Disorientation is a loss of self and/or object image clarity with sensory and motor capacities intact, but often unrelated

to time, place, person (name identity). (5) Unconsciousness is near total loss of awareness or perception.(6) The "Magnificent Feeling" or "Oceanic Feeling" is that state of consciousness where a person calmly recognizes truthfulness as an "equilibrium of awareness of self and environment with sensory and emotional harmony of self to the environment. This feeling can be psychical, as opposed to real, when inadequate attempts are made to determine truthful "identifications". Truthful identifications result from multiple, acceptable axes or sources of perception. The "Magnificent Feeling" reflects reality only to the degree that it represents emotions derived from truthful perception. It can be achieved with fantasy but results, in that case, in "rude awakenings". When associated with fantasy, the "Oceanic Feeling" is "Mysticism". But, when associated with a true perception of nature, beyond the usual perception, the "Oceanic Feeling" is "Transcendentalism". This author disagrees with Parsons6in his use of the word "Mysticism" in his description of Rolland's perceptive experience of the "Oceanic Feeling" (and Freud) in that Rolland relates his "Feeling" to a real experience of nature that is beyond the usual feeling obtained in a sensual experience. The "Feeling" is the "Feeling" of "Unity with the Universe"!

This "free association" or "free conceptualization" is fun and productive. It is the way our minds are creative. Imagine a piece of graph paper with squares. Make a large square composed of many small squares. The large square is a wave model. One of the small squares is a particle model. Think of each particle (EAD) as a small square and the wave for a given atom as one small square after the other in time, possibly 10^{15} per second, as a photon. Each successive wave contains many particles, numbered by the frequency of the wave. Frequency of electromagnetic waves can be measured with a spectroscope. The frequency unit of energy is the EAD and its energy value equals Planck's constant (h). The wave frequency number f times h equals a photon of Einstein. So, the wave and particle of energy are observed and recognized as to quality and quantity. The smallest units of perception may have been observed, but not named due to "state of consciousness" of the observers. The AMD is this author's name for the smallest unit of perception. These letters stand for Anne Mayberry Davis. She is my mother. The AMD may have the same "identity" as the "EAD". In a separate "paper", "Psychoanalysis

– Seeing Through the Reality Principle to Find Psychic Reality For the Narcissistic (Personality) Disorders", the probable relationship of frequency to sensory perception was explored. Truth is the integration of multiple true "subpercepts" of energies of different forms or "states", such as hearing, vision, touch, pressure, smell, so that the integration represents "reality" as seen by the "truthful observer". The "subpercepts" are subdivisions of Freud's "percept", an entity this author identifies with an integrated view of a given situation identified as to place and time. Between the "percept" and the "subpercepts" is **The Constant Subpercept of the core value system** of the "object" understudy. It **is the integrating factor or superego**. Also, "subpercepts" are divided as to perceptual quality by frequency of sensation per unit of receptor surface. So, it appears The AMD is the EAD after the EAD has been "transferred" to the cellular receptor. Thus, two names are needed because a "transformation" has occurred, as to "state". The EAD effects the cell receptor site to become an AMD, which then initiates neuron intracellular conduction pathways. Human perception is initiated by stimuli from the human's "id instincts" which cause it to interact or focus consciousness on outside sources for fulfillment of those instinctual needs. The environment, principally the primary caretaker, responds to the human child's stimuli to caretaker in a positive (loving or fulfilling) or negative (hateful, frustrating) way. The child develops "magnificent feelings" of love (due to truthfulness to his/her needs) or hate and emptiness due to frustration. The verbal description "associated" with this activity becomes the "superego" or "ego instincts" for survival by "compulsively associating" future objects in the phenomenon known as "transference".

Anne Elizabeth Mayberry Davis was a loving, primary caretaker who suggested truthfulness as an "ideal self". The author hopes he is perceived that way. Truthfulness is the source of his hope. This author's perceptual cycle is presented.

References to Chapter XI:

1 Sandler, Joseph; Rosenblatt, Bernard (1962). "The Concept of the Representational World". Psychoanalytic Study of the Child 17: 128-145 (135). 2 Sandler, Joseph; Holder, Alex; Meers, Dale (1963). "The Ego Ideal and the Ideal Self". Psychoanalytic Study of the Child 18: 139-158 (155).

3 Rolland, Romain (1881, 1882) as presented in his Nobel Prize (1915) winning book, **Jean Christophe** (1912).

4 Freud, Sigmund (1930). "**Civilization and It's Discontents**", S.E. 21: 59-145.

5 Bach, Sheldon. (1977). "On the Narcissistic State of Consciousness". International Journal of Psychoanalysis 58: 209-233 (523).

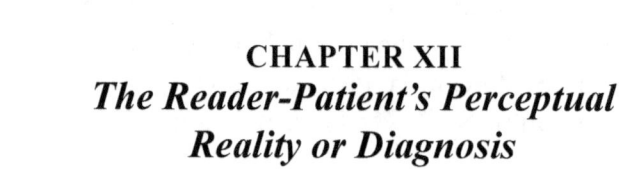

CHAPTER XII
The Reader-Patient's Perceptual Reality or Diagnosis

Well, the reader has an overwhelming amount of information! To make a diagnosis for the author's situation, the reader might perceive a "split", in that the author seems to "over idealize" and "devaluate" Professor Albert Einstein. The author suggests, as a proactive "defense", that the true ego of his friend is THE EQUATION that expresses The Secret of this universe "in the simple formality" of an equation and that it took a "synthesis" of this great man's "split" personality to find the "real" Professor Albert Einstein. The split professor is $E = Mc^2$. That seems like quite an accomplishment without "synthesis". The author has attempted to show you your universe. Is he truthful? Does the author, or the analysts, have a disorder? What's your diagnosis?

Question from the readers: "Before we make our individual diagnoses, tell us, simply, how you solved the puzzle." Well, the puzzle was to write in the "simple formality of an equation", or "identity", The Secret of the Universe. Einstein had exhibited a "devalued" self-image. His focus of consciousness was light. That meant he had an "over idealized" object-image of light. This directed attention to light, particularly the "photon" as to "identity". The photon was "over idealized" in terms of energy. This meant frequency was "devalued". The photon is actually a wave or "over idealized". The EAD is made necessary, because the journal Nature refused a paper redefining Einstein's "particle" of light. To avoid "Confusion of Tongues", the new term is mandated. The true "identities" of the wave and particle where "lost". This was a "Paradise Lost". Albert never lost his belief in God. He lost himself. Einstein lost his own, known truth of light. From reader-patients, "Dr. Davis, can you tell us the shortcut way to make a diagnosis of schizophrenia? You suggest the analysts might say you have schizophrenia or psychosis." Well, Bleuler (not Freud's Breuer) said there are four A's of schizophrenia. The first A is "loose association". Editor-analysts may attempt to say this author's association of the fantasy worlds with superego is "loose association", while he maintains he has observed it as a true association and that it is a true association that they have not made. Their failure to make this true association is just as grave an error as the making of untrue or false associations. In fact their association of behavior with the "Oedipal complex" is often a "loose association". The second A is "ambivalence". The editor-analysts might say the author's persistent presentation of similar "papers" to them is a sign of "ambivalence", suggesting that he does not care whether his "papers" are published or not. Actually, he feels this persistence is a sign of commitment to get this finding of: Fantasy World = Superego-Ego Complex (for pathology) and True World-view = Superego-ego Complex (for healthy, synthesized personality), recognized as a true identity and they, the editor-analysts, exhibit "ambivalence", or lack of commitment to their science, by not considering this finding in terms of their prior literature. This author points out this identity as a shared or "collective unconscious" of the editor-analysts or one of the denials of their "collective consciousness". The third A is "autism". Instead of accepting the emotional response of the editor-analysts to his "papers", this author has continued to follow a lonely course of persistent presentation of his "papers" to the editor-analysts. This might suggest to them that this author is "autistic", self-directed, or introverted relative to them. It might suggest to them that he is dissociated with them, because he does not accept their "collective consciousness". Whereas, to this author, looking for the truth in their literature, he is associative with the literature which reflects his observation of the fantasy world = superego-ego complex identity and dissociated with their behavior when it does not uphold the truthfulness of their literature that expresses his observation of true associations, as opposed to false alliances. Thus the author of this book views them as dissociated from their own literature by duplicity, or "autistic" (self-oriented). The fourth A is inappropriate "affect". The editor-analysts undoubtedly "feel" that it is "inappropriate" for this author to continue to present "papers" to them that challenge their lack of solution of the structural, developmental, and psychic energy conservation problems of the personality disorders. The perception of this author is, "The editor-analysts' 'affect' or 'feeling' is 'inappropriate' unless the editor-analysts have the solution to this problem and it is not the identity presented by this author." But, of course, the reader-patients are asking questions probably answerable by more "neutral" sources, such as DSM IV. The reader should recognize use of DSM IV as similar to the suggestion that Freud use the "Ten Commandments" to evaluate Moses and should find no problem with it, unless the reader (or Freud) wishes to propose other criteria and "stand up" for them. The American Psychiatric Association has given us criteria of diagnoses1. This is an honest expression of their opinion of disorders. When applied to all persons, including their members, these criteria are said to give true diagnoses by application of true descriptions of behavior to known associations of behavior with disorders. The reader-patient might now ask, "Who do you want us to diagnose?" The author responds, "Well everyone, of course. But in this particular defined universe, of a book, diagnose the editor-analysts, Professor Einstein, Wolfgang Pauli, the author, and yourself. The reason you must diagnose your "self" or define your ego is because it is the standard of value you use to diagnose everyone else. Recognize that your diagnoses and behavior will tell, all truly perceptive people, what you are! Your projection of self as to behavior and perception is your perceptual reality or ego in action and will be seen as your spirit or personality. The reader-patients now might say, "Well, now, we are not sure we want to be responsible for a diagnosis!" The author's response is, "This game is not voluntary. You must have perceptual reality to be conscious. **The important factor is the value system of your perception**. Is it to be a truthful value system or one of fantasy and denial? Lighten up! All you have to do is 'walk the chalk line'. The book is nearly over, so you must make a diagnosis. Analyses cannot go on forever. Analyses that are 'interminable' are stopped without resolution. This matter is going to be resolved in the 'here and now'. The author and the reader-patient willhave a perceptual reality. To suggest 'emptiness' is to be defensive of duplicity. Further questions would seem to be defensive in nature." The reader-patients might still ask further, "Can you give us a clue?" "Yes, assign truth, fantasy, or psychosis to each person in each situation. Remember, truth is not relative to the observer, it is reality. Also, truth, for any instant, relates to the material facts of that instant and should not be prejudiced by prior perceptions, which may have been incorrect." The reader chooses his or her own life with his diagnosis of the author, self, and others, as to truth. Everyone's life's experience relates to his own level of consciousness over time. The highest level of consciousness is "walking in the spirit" of truth. God bless you and your "objects", or "subjects" (as to study).

Reference to Chapter XII:

1 American Psychiatric Association's **Diagnostic and Statistical Manual IV**. Fourth Edition, 1400 K Street, N.W., Washington, D.C., 2005.

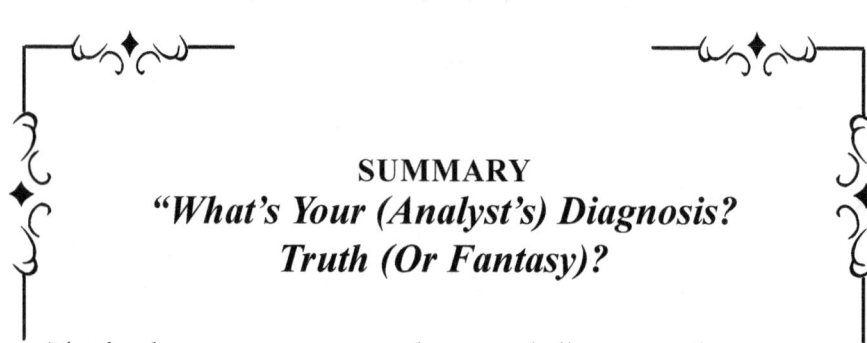

SUMMARY
"What's Your (Analyst's) Diagnosis?
Truth (Or Fantasy)?

This book presents answers to the most challenging and controversial problems of psychoanalysis, ethicssocial science, and physics in its solution of the questions of structural development of personality, "free will", and the "unified field" of physics. It might not surprise the well educated that Albert Einstein anticipated that these solutions would be part of a unified whole of perception "apart from humanity". These answers are consistent with the greater world-views (or total consciousness) of Freud, Einstein, and Jesus of Nazareth. The editors of journals of "normal science" do not accept them, for publication, because acceptance would mandate finding truth instead of feeling that truth (reality) is self (a part of perceived humanity). Self, as an "ideal self" of "truth", is unreal or "apart from humanity", just as Einstein said. Finding the answers to these different, but related, questions has been a great challenge. Getting these answers published, except at personal expense, has been impossible, to date. Reader(s) should recognize that editors of the most prestigious journals of "normal science" have denied them access to the reading of these solutions just as the U.S. Supreme Court denies U.S. children access to religious education in the public schools of the U.S. The motive appears to be the same, in both cases, separation of self from the real (spiritual) world by denial of its' reality in the self. This book suggests "truth" is not real unless it is "generally" (randomly and universally) applicable and that the "self" is not alive unless truthful. It does, explicitly, recognize untruthful or negative, personalities and negative situations in its positive or truthful reality perception.

Solution of the question of structural development of personality, as separate from the genetic person, is just as Freud said it is. The world-view of perception and value for action of the personality is that person's superego or "character" as developed in the value system of the primary relationship(s).

The question of "free will" relates to the presence or absence of truthfulness as the core value of one's character or superego. Discovery that "free will" results from making the preconscious mind conscious is a development of recognition that forcing the value system to be truthfulness requires conscious awareness of the value system. This insight occurred simultaneously with the author's recognition of the reason why his answers were not accepted for publication by the "normal science" journals and is validated by their use of classic "defense mechanisms" (use of statements that are provably untrue and, even if true, are inadequate to meet the needs of the situation).

While Freud found the solution to the personality's development, he could not be conscious that he had done so, due to the "split of his ego in the process of defense" where he presented personality development as both superego and Oedipal complex, clearly a duplicitous state of thought (science) that resulted from failure to identify the personality as separate from the genetic person. Similarly, Einstein's "split" of consciousness, of the same cause, denied him the solution of the "unified field". The author's recognition of Einstein's "devalued" selfimage led to recognition of Einstein's "over-idealized" perceptual image of light as a "particle" (photon).

Once these truths were established, the behavior of editors was observed as personalities-in-action relative to these determined truths. The behavior of these editors, as well as publication of these truths, is the subject and plot of this book. In this manner, this book explains the cost of lack of truthfulness as the core value of "character" or personality, almost, as well as a closely analyzed soap opera. That cost is suggested as death of the self as a real person. After all, reality is truth, by definition.

The personality, or spirit of our relationship to others, is our superego value system. It is integrated as the ego or self-image in the primary relationship by the "identification" process of the child, with a relationship that values, most highly, a certain trait that is discovered to determine a person's value by the dominant person's conceptualization of the primary relationship. Pathology of the personality results from "identification" with false reality perception as determined by false conceptualization of the primary relationship. "Free will" is our ability to choose truth and reality as opposed to lies or fantasy. It is actually developed, like a muscle, by forcing the self to be truthful. The cure of the "Sinful Man" syndrome is for the sinful man to choose truthfulness, as Christ, and others, have recommended.

The "Unified Field Theory" of Albert Einstein is named, in this book, the "Unified Field Theory of 'Charged Particle' Relations and Mass-Energy Transformation(s)". The "Equation of Mass-Energy Transformation(s)" is given and the unit of transformation, the EAD, is extensively "identified". Failure to reach the unified field, before, resulted from lack of true "identification" of the unit of mass-energy-charge transformation. The unit quantity of energy of transformation is Planck's constant expressed as energy, not h energy multiplied by frequency. Recognition of the inverse relationship of energy, rather than a direct "relative" relationship, to mass (matter) leads to the unity of all three physical theories, whereas Einstein envisioned the unity of gravitational and electromagnetic. For this author, the "Unified Field Theory" of Albert Einstein is established as a true fact of reality or nature. (But, not for the journal *Nature*.) This fact is a testament or tribute to the soul of Albert Einstein and his truthfulness as a human (imperfect) personality. Gravitation (with inertia), atomic, and electromagnetic theories are unified. There is a variable field, dependent on distance from mass, with direction, dependent on that mass's center and its direct or indirect relationship to charge, energy, mass, force, acceleration, position, velocity, frequency, period, wavelength, The Equation is:

(For the atom(s)): $\Delta^{Mc2} = \Delta E = EADn \times -EADe = EADn \times EADm \times c^2 = EADn \times +/-EADc$ at velocity c (dependent upon direction + towards a given mass or location in question)= (For Gravity): $1/2(G((M1M2/d1^2) + (M1_\Delta M2_\Delta/d2^2))) \times \Delta^d$ = (For Electromagnetism): $1/2(K((q1q2/d1^2) + (q1_\Delta q2_\Delta/d2^2))) \times \Delta d$ For Gravity and Electromagnetism Δd is positive when decreasing. Perception of the EAD1 as a "particle" is intuitively apparent when thought of as "mass" or "charge". But when the EAD1 is thought of as energy, it is intuitively perceived as a "wave", even though it is only one "particle". This results from "reality" apart from the "normal" human perception of the senses and previously conceptualized or "normal science".

APPENDEX[1]
The Davis Constants for: "The Unified Field Theory of 'Charged Particle' Relations and Mass-Energy Transformation"
and The Unified Field Theory Equation

The following table of constants and their calculations are to be copyrighted, separately from this book, where they are explained and developed in fuller detail than in this copyrighted appendix. These constants are required for quantitative understanding and use of the "Unified Field Theory of 'Charged Particle' Relations and Mass-Energy Transformation" with its associated equation: "**The Unified Field Theory Equation**":

(For the atom(s)): $\Delta Mc^2 = \Delta E$ = EADn x -EADe = EADn x EADm x c^2 =+/- EADn x EADc at velocity c (dependent upon + as direction towards a mass or location in question) = (For Gravity): $^{1/2}$(G((M1M2/d1^2) + (M1ΔM2Δ/d2^2))) x Δd = (For Electromagnetism): $^{1/2}$(K((q1q2/d1^2) + (q1Δq2Δ/d2^2))) x Δd For Gravity and Electromagnetism Δd is positive when decreasing. Perception of the EAD1 as a "particle" is intuitively apparent when thought of as "mass" or "charge". But when the EAD1 is thought of as energy, it is intuitively perceived as a "wave", even though it is only one "particle". EADn is the number of particles of energy transformed. The "EADe" is the initials of the name given to the smallest unit of electromagnetic energy. Its energy is similar to Planck's constant or 6.626 X 10-^{34} Joules. To obtain a mass equivalent: h = Mc2 or M = h/c2 = "EADm" = 7.37241927 X 10-51Kg. To obtain the charge per "EADc": Charge = energy/voltage change = 6.626 X 10-^{34} Joules/ 4.1361 X 10-^{15} electron volts per Coulomb = +1.6022 X 10-^{19} Coulombs. This "identifies" the EAD as the positive electromagnetic "Particle" generated by electron motion during fusion. Of course, Albert Einstein suggested the "unified field" would be found when we understood the relationships or "relativity" of mass, charge, distance, time, and velocity. Velocity of the EAD is c (the speed of light and electromagnetic waves). Since the EAD is a charged particle in motion, it has two planes of vibration. The one in the direction of propagation is the electromotive wave associated with inertia and the one perpendicular to that propagation is the electromagnetic wave of gravity. It therefore has two waves, one perpendicular to the plane of motion, and one perpendicular to the plane of vibration. Velocity's direction is positive, for a given mass, when toward that mass and negative, when away from that mass. The reference point in space must be defined by unity or agreement of the observers, which then gives ability to have determinant times and positions for all observers.

Frequency of the EAD is determined by the nucleus of its source and is measurable by spectrophotometer. It is the number of "particles" of light or electromagnetic waves passing a point per second. Wavelength is the distance between particles in space in the plane perpendicular to propagation and depends on intensity of EAD particles (light particles) due to Brownian motion of light particles and limited space related to the limit of c (the speed of light). The magnetic wavelength is determined by the "mass" source (Sun) and its intensity of energy production. There is equilibrium between energy production and energy consumption related to mass of the producing star.

"Mutual Atomic-Molecular Polarity"

The unifying concept of the phenomena of gravity and inertia is "Mutual Atomic-Molecular Polarity". The force fields of gravity and inertia result from the fact that all charges, regardless of distance, exert force upon all other charges. Prior to the acceptance of this concept, inertia is not explained and gravity is explained as "a deformation of space by mass". Recognition of atomic-molecular polarity, resulting from the charges of particles in masses gives explanation of both gravity and inertia. This is application of Maxwell's theories and wave equations. It is expression of disagreement with Einstein's "relativity" perception of Maxwell's work. The author is aware of the fact that Albert Einstein used a charged rod in his studies of "bodies in motion". This suggests the scientific community will accept use of a charged rod in further studies of "neutral masses". This author has pictures taken of two magnets at the ends of a metal rod oriented in magnetic east-west direction. These pictures show the north poles of both magnets pointing to their respective ends of the metal rod. This is evidence that "Mutual Atomic-Molecular Polarity", "MAMP", occurs in a metal rod due to local charge conditions. These pictures and this experiment took place before the author read Professor Einstein's paper on "The Electrodynamics of Moving Bodies"2. This author agrees with the professor that charged wires or magnetized compasses are acceptable instruments to study gravity and inertia as related to charges in the masses. Clark presents the compass as one of Albert Einstein's favorite instruments. This author is also fascinated with compasses and has at least three of them. Use of more than one compass is necessary to perceive, by experiment, "Mutual Atomic-Molecular Polarity", unless you accept the phenomenon of gravity as proof of "Mutual Atomic-Molecular Polarity" or you can design another experiment to demonstrate this point. To this author, "deformation of space", without a physical force explanation, is simply inadequate. This author gives a physical force explanation that explains both gravity and inertia. Einstein has not given us the necessary physical force mechanisms for gravity or inertia, two real physical phenomena. Readers are, therefore, required to accept this explanation, derived from the well-accepted Maxwell theory, or provide a better one that does not relate inversely related phenomena. Einstein has not given a mechanism for his "deformation of space by mass" and he has not explained inertia.

"Charge to Mass Equivalence for Neutral Masses":

The derivation of this constant results from the use of a "Unity Equation" or recognition that "things equal to equal things are equal to each other". Thus, when gravity is found to exist and result from "MAMP" or "effective charge", the charge can be calculated by equating the gravitational and Coulomb equations.

Calculation of "The Charge to Mass Ratio of Neutral Masses"

To get "The Charge to Mass Ratio of Neutral Masses", the situation is first recognized as an "identity" or "equivalent" property of mass to be a charge dependent property because of the known presence of charges and their universal effects upon other charges. The shape of molecules and their proton-electron charge-to-wave relationships co-relates the electron waveforms and proton charge position of atoms to the molecule as a single mass. These same electron waveforms of molecules and atoms relate the global particles of atoms and molecules to the universe of particles of "charges" by the waveform positions. There is therefore, a wave-form "parity" of each and every electron wave-form to the rest of the universe or its' summed or integrated charge position.

The forces of distant masses upon local masses relates to the waveforms generated by motion of their charged particles (electrons and protons) is proportional to the product of those masses (distant and local) and inversely proportional to the square of their separating distance. The **charges are very small** for "neutral masses"

(8.61646 X 10^{-11} Coulombs/Kg.).

Gk = 6.673 X 10-^{11} Newton meters squared/Kg^2 = F = 8.988 X 10^9NM^2/Coulombs^2 = Ck **1 Kg = 8.61646 X 10^{-11} Coulombs**

1 Coulomb = 1.16057 X 10^{10} Kg

Calculations of force in Newtons of gravity by Coulombs Law and charge-to-mass ratio for a 70 Kg. Man at the surface of the earth yields results within .248% of that for Newton's Law, for the 100 Kg. Man .337%, and for the Earth –Moon force the sameresult (although neither result the author got, 1.971 X 10^{20} Newtons, is the reference result of 2.1 X 10^{20} Newtons). The author recognizes the differences are due to different mass values used as reference standards for earth-moon force and the small errors resulting from minor multiplier effects of constants due to choice of significant figure number. The masses used by the author are: Earth 5.98 X 10^{24} Kg.; Moon 7.30 X 10^{22} Kg. The case for understanding these constants is well made in the book:

What's Your (Analyst's) Diagnosis? Table of Davis Constants: 1 "Particle" or Mass or Mass "Equivalent Mass" Charge Mass/Charge Ratio Charge/Mass Ratio

"Equivalent Energy"

"EAD" EADm EADc 4.6014 X **"Particle" 7.37241927 + 1.6022** 10-^{32} "EADn" X X Kg./Coul. 2.18175 X 10^{31} Coul./Kg. is Particle Number **10^{-51} 10^{-19}** Kg. **"(Kd)"** Copyrighted 03-05-05 Coulombs EADe 6.626 X 10^{-34} Joules Or 8.98755178737 X 10^{16} Joules/kg. **Photon "wave"** Frequency (f) (hf) EADm X Frequency (f) EADc X EAD Same as EAD Same as 6.626 X 10^{-34} Joules X Frequency **hf** Electron Charged "Particle" With Wave Form X 9.109 X 10^{-31} Kg. -1.6022 X 10^{-19} Coulombs 5.6853 X 10^{-12} Kg./Coulomb 1.7589 X 10^{11} Coul./Kg. Proton Charged "particle" With Wave Form 1.673 X 10^{-27} Kg. + 1.6022 X 10^{-19} Coulombs 1.04419 X 10^{-8} Kg./Coulomb 9.5768 X 10^7 Coulombs/Kg. "Neutral Mass" – Kg. 1.00000n Kg. 1.16057 X 1010 Kg./Coulomb **"MAMP" "Effective Charge"** 8.61646 X 10^{-11} Coulombs/ Kg.(Dc) Energy at c 8.98755178737 X 10^{16} Joules

To check the calculation: 1.0 kg. / (7.37241927 X 10^{-51} kg.) X 6.626 X 10^{-34} Joules = 8.987551789 X 10^{16} Joules. **The Unity Unit of Mass-Energy Relationships** is established as the **EAD**.

References to the Appendix: 1 NOTE: The constants used to derive these constants came from Merrill (1995) **Physics** – Principles and Problems (P712 and 408) by Paul Zitzewitz, Robert Neff, and Mark Davids. Glencoe/McGraw-Hill, N.Y., N.Y. 2 Einstein, Albert (1905). "On the Electrodynamics of Moving Bodies". Annalen der **Physik 17: 891-921.**

Author's Page

Frank E. Davis, III., M.D., FACS

Born: Baltimore, Maryland, 3-20-1947. Lived in Grifton, N.C. 1953-1965. Grifton was a great small town (of approximately 1800 people) to grow up in! The author loved hunting quail, squirrels, and deer, as well as playing baseball and football. A mentor the author had in baseball, Howard Crest, later became the plant manager at Dupont. His character was appreciated long before he had such great success.

College – University: U.N.C. is the home of James Taylor, whose father (Montrose) was the dean of my medical school. We met at the end-of-year medical school party 1972. This author loves "Carolina" just as much as James Taylor. University of North Carolina, Chemistry (A.B.), 1969, M.D. 1973 Surgical P. G. 1 and 2 Hospital of University of Pennsylvania 1973-1975 Chief Resident in Surgery Eastern Virginia Medical School 1978-1979 Diplomate American Board of Surgery 1980, 1990, 2000 Physics Teacher, Williamston High School 2002-2003 Member of the American Association for the Surgery of Trauma

Acknowledgments

First, my mother has shared my struggle with the psychoanalysts and helped me to understand their perception, or lack of it. She has been very tolerant of my "split" presence in her home as I developed my perception of personality development and self. I am reminded of a time when I was reading Honore'Balzac's fictional works about personality and was, psychically, in Paris. My mother asked me a question that I did not consciously hear. She then, humorously said, "Oh, that's right, you're in Paris!" She is a dear, dear soul. Her leadership led me to give up on the psychoanalysts and avoid further time loss with presentations to the physicists.

Second, I owe a great deal of respect and thanks to the librarians who have assisted me in my search of the medical literature in a field of medicine apart from my specialty. Jean Christopher Blackwell of the U.N.C. Health Sciences Library and Vicki Daughtridge of the Laupus Library of the E.C.U. Brody School of Medicine have been graciously helpful. The works of Melanie Klein and Sigmund Freud were watersheds of information given to me by these librarians.

The permissions process was very moving to this author, as most permissions were granted without charge. Especially revealing were the gracious grants of permission by Dr. William Parsons, Dr. Sheldon Bach, as well as, Elizabeth Clementson of W.W. Norton for **The Standard Edition of the Complete Works of Sigmund Freud.** It is also a pleasure to acknowledge here, as requested, that the Piaget translations concerning a true "logic of relations" are presented from **Factors Determining Human Behavior: Harvard Tercentenary Conference of Arts and Sciences,** by Edgar Douglas Adrian, et al., Cambridge, Mass.: Harvard University Press, Copyright 1937 by the President and Fellows of Harvard College.

Finally, and associated with most direct and timely help is the staff of the Halifax Community College E.R.C., where the word processing was done. Great assistance was required and given by Brian Lassister and Don Worrock.

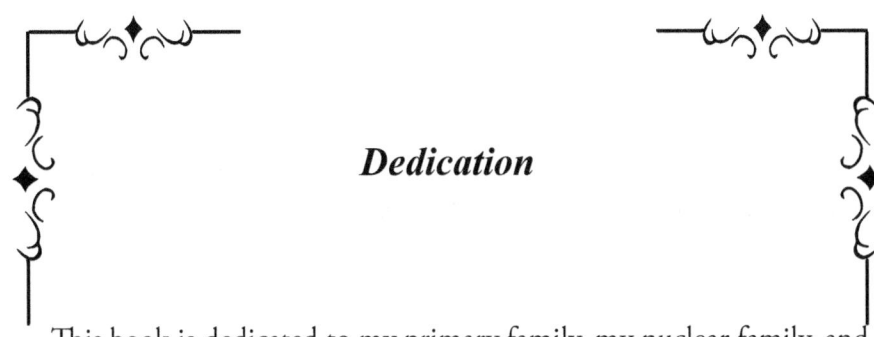

Dedication

This book is dedicated to my primary family, my nuclear family, and the world, a great and joyous place to live.

Primary Family:

Father: Frank E. Davis, Jr. This man was a person who knew you could not get energy ("anything") "for nothing". He knew how to love truthfully. He was, to this author, gifted and is believed to have had an I.Q. of 165. He valued education, formal and informal, and expressed a desire to "write a book" and "be a doctor". He, my sister, and I had great joy at my expense once when the "little moron jokes" were in vogue. My mentor, sister, had been bringing "little moron jokes" home from school, when I was four years old. I found them so funny, then, that I would roll in the floor with laughter when Ann Lynn told one. My father delighted in this brother-sister bonding, but did not like it that I found stupidity in others so funny. One day, while he was at work, he thought of a way to teach me a lesson. When he came home, he got Ann Lynn and I to come to him and said, "Ann Lynn, Sandy, your mother and I were born in North Carolina. So, we are called North Carolinians. Since you were born in Baltimore, what would you be called?The author blurted out, "Baltimorons!" My father was not showing his "brilliance" at my expense. He was teaching me to respect even morons, maybe, especially morons.

Mother: Anne Elizabeth Mayberry Davis. Born in Rocky Mount, N.C. A dedicated, loving, and truthful mother, who "transferred" her core, paternal-relationship value to me. Her father died just prior to my birth. To psychoanalysts, this means she "recathected" her id energy for him to me in the "mourning" process. Truthfulness was the spirit of her relationship with her father. You could say that that "feeling" for truthfulness, as a conceptualization of self, has been transferred from my grandfather, Walter Linzy Mayberry, to me, as if by genes.

Sister: Ann Lynn Davis Grant was my mentor, in my primary years, for my recognition of the world as a place with different values than that of our family. I seem to have gotten more perception, as to how the world works, from my sister than from my parents and in this manner kept the home world and the "real world" separate. This is not to imply that my sister is worldly, but to give the reader knowledge of my sister's value to me in perceiving the world, realistically. Her perception is effective as "she lives in a big white house and is married to a doctor!" I love her, her husband, her children, their spouses, and her grandchildren with deep feeling.

Sister: Jeva Mayberry Davis Jones is a sensitive, giving caretaker of young children. I would surely entrust my child to her care! She and I have shared some worldly experiences better left in the unconscious. But, they have brought us closer together and given us a shared identity. Her husband, Ervin, is a "brother".

Nuclear Family:

Wife: Lauren Anne Walker Davis has been a very charming, exciting, and challenging mate. She has been an exceptionally dedicated mother. I love her, though we are apart. What's Your (Analyst's) Diagnosis? Truth (or Fantasy)?

Daughter: Elizabeth Anne Davis (EAD) is the most valued extension of my life. She is verbally gifted, very attractive, academically successful, athletically talented, and emotionally sensitive. Like all young people, she will find emotional perception with experience. This author loves her, more than life, and he is well pleased with her as a person of great value. If everything this author does could be dedicated to one person, it would be to her. But, his spirit, and soul, have always been dedicated to truthfulness and he hopes she can see that as in the best interest of everyone, especially her. EAD's choice of institution of higher education, Virginia Military Institute – V.M.I., is a testament of her values of truthfulness and integrity. Her ability to realize those values grows with her use of them. She is deeply valued, respected, and loved for that effort. But, her soul is treasured, despite any disagreement and, in all perception.